Your Towns and Cities in the Great War

❖

mfriesshire
in the Great War

This book is dedicated to those whose lives were changed by the First World War

Your Towns and Cities in the Great War

Dumfriesshire
in the Great War

Timothy McCracken

Pen & Sword
MILITARY

First published in Great Britain in 2015 by
PEN & SWORD MILITARY
an imprint of
Pen and Sword Books Ltd
47 Church Street
Barnsley
South Yorkshire S70 2AS

ISBN 9781473823075

Printed and bound in England
by CPI Group (UK) Ltd, Croydon, CR0 4YY

Typeset in Times New Roman

Pen & Sword Books Ltd incorporates the imprints of
Pen & Sword Archaeology, Atlas, Aviation, Battleground, Discovery,
Family History, History, Maritime, Military, Naval, Politics, Railways,
Select, Social History, Transport, True Crime, and Claymore Press,
Frontline Books, Leo Cooper, Praetorian Press, Remember When,
Seaforth Publishing and Wharncliffe.
For a complete list of Pen and Sword titles please contact
Pen and Sword Books Limited
47 Church Street, Barnsley, South Yorkshire, S70 2AS, England
E-mail: enquiries@pen-and-sword.co.uk
Website: **www.pen-and-sword.co.uk**

Contents

Cover photograph: Members of the 34th Voluntary Aid Detachment (Dumfries) with patients, outside Langholm Red Cross Hospital. Two patients in Royal Army Medical Corps (RAMC) uniform can be identified sitting at front of the group as they have round Red Cross badges on their sleeves.
Courtesy of Ms Caroline Brisbane-Jones-Stamp

Acknowledgements

Ms Janice Aitken for permission to include photographs

Mr Bryan Armstrong and Mr William Laidlaw, Dumfriesshire Newspaper Group, Annan, for access to the newspaper group archives and permission to include photographs

Ms Caroline Brisbane-Jones-Stamp for permission to include photographs

Sir John Buchanan-Jardine, Bt., for permission to include photographs

Mr David Calvert for permission to include extracts from the diary of John Corrie and permission to include photographs

Mr Glen Carr whose school history teaching provided an excellent foundation for further study

Mr Duncan Close for research advice and permission to include photographs

Professor Karl-Erik Frandsen whose teaching at the University of Copenhagen provided excellent guidance in developing research skills

Ms Barbara Janman for research advice and permission to include photographs

Mr Peter John for research advice

Mr Ian Martin, The King's Own Scottish Borderers Museum, Berwick-upon-Tweed, for research advice and permission to include photographs

Ms Brenda Morrison, and the Langholm Archive Group, for permission to include photographs

Mr Derek Robertson for research advice and permission to include photographs

Dr Thomas Rohkrämer and Dr Alan Warburton, whose excellent seminars at Lancaster University provided detailed insight into the social impacts of the First World War

The staff of the Dumfries and Galloway Libraries, Information and Archive Service, Ewart Library, Dumfries, for research advice and permission to include photographs

The British Red Cross Museum and Archives, London, for research advice

Introduction

IN DUMFRIESSHIRE, as throughout the United Kingdom, and indeed in all the nations involved in the conflict, the First World War had a great impact.

There was no common personal experience of the conflict with an individual, perhaps amongst many events and feelings, experiencing the loss of family and friends, fear, a desire to support the war effort and grief following the end of the conflict. It is hoped the aspects explored in this study will help to illustrate some of the experiences, shaped by the First World War, of the population of Dumfriesshire.

Dumfriesshire is a rural border county situated in the south-west of Scotland, separated from England by the Solway Firth. Today the county forms part of Dumfries and Galloway which was created in 1975 with the unification of Dumfriesshire and Galloway, as a result of the Local Government (Scotland) Act 1973.

In 1911 Dumfriesshire had a population of 72,825. Three principal rivers run through the county; the Nith, Annan, and Esk run from north to south, their valleys providing

Sketch map of Dumfriesshire parish boundaries and burghs

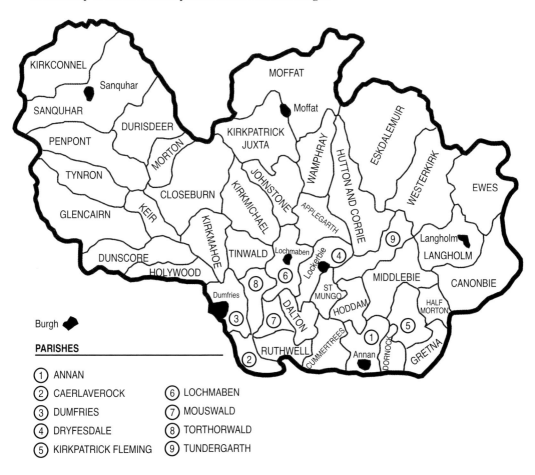

road routes to central Scotland. By the early years of the twentieth century an extensive system of railways provided the main means of transport within the county and to outlying areas. Carlisle, just south of Dumfriesshire and the Scottish Border, was an important railway junction, with main lines running to Edinburgh, Glasgow and Stranraer.

The major centre of population was Dumfries; in 1911 the town had a population of 16,011. It was not until 1929 the burgh of Maxwelltown united with Dumfries to form one burgh.

As the county town, Dumfries had a great variety of trades, shops and services available. These included five aerated water manufacturers, eleven watch and clock makers, thirty-eight milliners and dressmakers, twenty-one tobacconists, twenty hotels, twenty-two tailors and clothiers and forty-three wine and spirit merchants. The town's progress since the 1890s ensured that by 1911 the streets were lit by electricity.

In 1911 the provincial towns in the region all had populations considerably smaller than Dumfries, their combined number of inhabitants not totalling that of Dumfries. Annan had a population of 4,219; Langholm, 2,930; Lochmaben, 1,056; Lockerbie 2,455; Moffat, 2,079; and Sanquhar 1,508. Less diverse than Dumfries, the towns still had a considerable variety of trades, one of the most specialised being that of wine and spirit merchant. There were five in Annan, four in Moffat, three in Lockerbie and two in Langholm. Sanquhar did not have a listed wine and spirit merchant, but did have the services of a spirit dealer.

Prior to the outbreak of the First World War the Dumfriesshire economy was largely dominated by agriculture, with coal mined around Canonbie, Kirkconnel and Sanquhar and lead mined in the Wanlockhead area. The rural areas of the region were extensively used for farming. The upland northern areas were suitable for sheep farming, the river valleys and coastal plains used for both dairy and arable farming. Agriculture formed the greatest industry in the county; the area's towns provided markets for the produce.

However the region also had some light manufacturing industries prior to the outbreak of war, with some factories later adapting to war work. The Arrol-Johnston motor company came to Dumfries in 1912. During the First World War production at the factory switched to aero engines, propellers, frames and machine gun parts, the number of employees increasing from 500 in 1914 to a peak of 1,500. During the winter of 1914, due to a combination of government orders and the enlistment of employees in the armed forces, Arrol-Johnston experienced a labour shortage. A considerable number of openings for those ineligible for military service were noted.

In the Dumfries textile mills production also changed during the conflict. At Rosefield and Troqueer mills production switched to khaki and French army blue cloth for the Allied armies, and at MacGeorge's Mill manufacture changed to army gloves.

As throughout the United Kingdom in 1914, refugees were welcomed to Dumfriesshire. A group of nineteen French refugees arrived, who had been occupants of a convent in Belgium, a short distance from the French border. They arrived in London from Ostend and British friends then arranged their travel to Dumfries by rail, where they were going to reside in Dumfries Convent.

In late September 1914 an estimated one hundred Belgian refugees were expected to arrive in Lower Annandale, and were to be temporarily accommodated in village halls until homes and work could be found for them.

In the autumn of 1914 some of the refugees who arrived first were accommodated in Beattock and Lockerbie. Ten arrived at Lockerbie Station and were met by Mr David McJerrow, Town Clerk, and Madame Ost, a Belgian lady. The following day they travelled to their accommodation in Johnstone parish. In this group there were two men, three women and five children from Malines and Bruges. Both men had been wounded and their homes completely destroyed. A local committee arranged the furnishing of cottages and money was guaranteed for the refugees' subsistence until the end of the war.

A family of ten from the Malines area was accommodated on the farm of Wyseby Mains, near Kirkpatrick Fleming. Mr Sloan, the proprietor of the farm, gave the family the use of two furnished cottages. Miss Mary Theresa Graham of Mossknowe, and Mrs Sloan of Wyseby Mains, ensured they had sufficient food and clothing.

In Annan a house in Lawson's Court, Greencroft Wynd was furnished for Belgian refugees by the Annan Relief Committee. After correspondence with the Glasgow Corporation Belgian Refugee Committee, two ladies from the Annan Relief Committee travelled to Glasgow to arrange for the return of refugees to Annan. Nine refugees arrived at Annan Station and were welcomed by members of the committee and the local Scouts, who assisted with the luggage. They were Monsieur Gilbert, with his wife and child, a baby of eight months, his two sisters and his young brother, Madame Gilbert's sister and two friends. Monsieur Gilbert was unable to serve in the military due to a leg injury. The Annan Relief Committee thanked the community for furniture, which was gifted and loaned. The Scouts assisted by collecting weekly donations of money from local subscribers.

By 1916 there were fourteen Belgian refugees under the care of the Annan Belgian Refugees' Committee: one elderly man, five women and eight children. One family residing in Victoria Road, Annan, had become entirely self-supporting and were able to pay their own rent. In December 1918, there was a large attendance at a bring-and-buy sale, held in the YMCA Institute, Annan, organised by the committee to provide financial aid to local refugees on their return home to Belgium which was expected soon after the sale.

Fourteen Belgian refugees, from Malines and Ostend, arrived from London at Ruthwell Station, to join those already accommodated in Dalton and Carrutherstown. From Ostend they had travelled to Calais by fishing boat, and had the terrible experience of being stranded on a sandbank for twelve hours. Employment on a farm was quickly found for some of the group.

At Westerkirk, near Langholm, six Belgian refugees arrived from Glasgow. They were one family, consisting of a father and mother, housed at Midpark, Westerhall and a widowed daughter with three children, housed in a recently completed cottage at Bentpath. The family came from Malines, the daughter being a costumier there until her shop was destroyed by shelling. Provision for their transport, accommodation and subsistence was made by Mr and Mrs Berkley Matthews and family of Westerhall.

Belgian refugees were also accommodated at Penpont. On arrival they were met at Thornhill Station and were accommodated in the house formerly used as the Temperance Hotel, placed at the disposal of the local relief committee by the Duke of Buccleuch. A number of local people contributed from four pence to four shillings monthly for their support, and arrangements for their reception were made by the Red Cross Society. Nearby, at Moniaive, two Belgian families arrived with thirteen young children between them. Both families travelled by train from Glasgow and were supported by public subscription. The Glencairn Belgian Relief Committee made arrangements for their stay.

At Moffat, during 1917–1918, the sum of £245 9s was raised in a variety of ways including donations, a concert and a jumble sale. In early 1918 nine Belgian refugees were accommodated at Dundanion. The Moffat Belgian Refugee Fund Committee thanked Mr Deane for allowing them to live there for so long rent-free.

A summary of the support provided to Belgian refugees in the parish of Morton was published in early 1918. From December 1914, the parish undertook entire responsibility for the maintenance of three families. Weekly door-to-door collections took place, for amounts varying from 1d to 1s. Initially a committee of ladies shopped for the Belgians, but after a few months the refugees had enough knowledge of the language to shop independently. They were given a weekly allowance which varied from 15s to 23s depending on the size of the family. The refugees were also supplied with boots and clothing and were regularly visited by Mrs Ralston, Mrs David Kirkpatrick and Mrs Paterson. For the period from 7 December 1914, when the first families came to Thornhill, until 31 December 1917, a sum of £449 4s 11d had been received through parish collections; during the period expenditure was £414 8s 6d. By early 1918, two cottages were occupied by the Belgian refugees at Burnbrae. In late 1917 the local Belgian Relief Committee thanked the local population for all the support received, and an appeal was made for continued financial support, as contributions had begun to decrease over the last year.

When the war ended refugees in the region returned to Belgium. Louis Feyaerts, and his daughter Louisa, returned to the Louvain area, where they had lived on a small croft. In autumn 1914 Mr Feyaerts' son was shot as he was leaving the house and, in the hurry of departure, his married daughter was left behind.

Louis Feyaerts and Louisa, worked for four years at Dormont Home Farm, Dalton. They were presented with gifts by Mr Morton, factor of Dormont, on behalf of the estate workers. Colonel and Mrs Carruthers, of Dormont House, also presented them with gifts. Arrangements for their journey home, and the shipment of their luggage, were carried out by Mr Morton.

Although the changes to some of the existing industries in the region resulted in secure demand during the war, and some increased employment, the major change was to occur at Gretna. Here the largest cordite factory in the UK was established, work commencing on the factory in 1915, with completion in 1916. Prior to 1915 most of the area was used as agricultural land, with three small villages, Gretna Green, Rigg and Springfield. Before the war the area was renowned for runaway marriages due to its close proximity to the English border. Gretna railway junction was important as the

A photograph of a representative group of Belgian refugees, who were assisted to find homes by arrangements made by Mrs Murray, Murraythwaite, and a network of friends, throughout Dumfriesshire. The first Belgian refugees arrived in autumn 1914, and were initially accommodated in halls in the Cummertrees and Ruthwell area. Most of the refugees returned home to Belgium, but some decided to remain in the United Kingdom.
Photograph courtesy of the Dumfriesshire Newspaper Group

main lines from Glasgow (via Beattock) and Stranraer (via Dumfries) met. The total population of the area in 1911 was 1,212, but rose to around 20,000 during the peak period in the war. The parish was to undergo the greatest changes in the area due to the war and the huge increase in population also had a significant impact on the surrounding area.

In addition to the Gretna munitions factory, perhaps during the First World War Dumfriesshire was most nationally known for the tragic Quintinshill Rail Disaster on 22 May 1915. The 1/7th Battalion Royal Scots (The Royal Regiment) was travelling to Liverpool on the way to Gallipoli. The troop train, travelling from the north, collided

The aftermath of the Quintinshill Rail Disaster. *Photograph courtesy of the Dumfriesshire Newspaper Group*

with a local passenger train, which had been moved onto the track to allow the London to Glasgow express to pass. The express then ran into the crash, causing more casualties. The Western Front Association Memorial, at Gretna Green, commemorates the 227 people who lost their lives in the disaster. Around a further 250 people were injured.

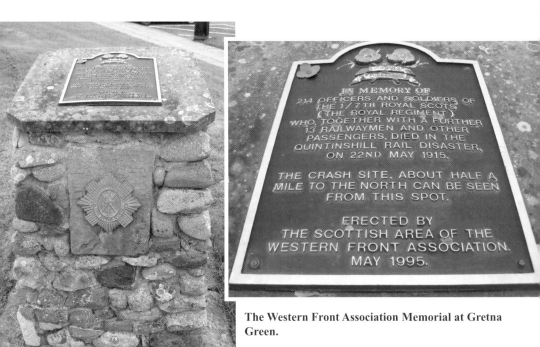

The Western Front Association Memorial at Gretna Green.

Stormont Hall, Gretna Green. The Caledonian Railway paid the Stormont Hall Committee to refurbish the floor, after the hall was used as a temporary mortuary for those killed in the disaster.

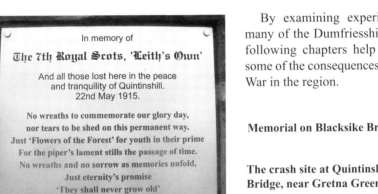

In memory of

The 7th Royal Scots, 'Leith's Own'

And all those lost here in the peace
and tranquility of Quintinshill.
22nd May 1915.

No wreaths to commemorate our glory day,
nor tears to be shed on this permanent way.
Just 'Flowers of the Forest' for youth in their prime
For the piper's lament stills the passage of time.
No wreaths and no sorrow as memories unfold,
Just eternity's promise
'They shall never grow old'

Words by
Denis Muir

Springfield & Gretna Green
Community Council 2009

By examining experiences shared by many of the Dumfriesshire population, the following chapters help in understanding some of the consequences of the First World War in the region.

Memorial on Blacksike Bridge.

The crash site at Quintinshill, from Blacksike Bridge, near Gretna Green.

Chapter 1

The 5th Battalion King's Own Scottish Borderers and recruitment

THE KING'S OWN SCOTTISH BORDERERS (KOSB) was the county regiment for Dumfriesshire on the outbreak of war in 1914. At this time the regiment consisted of two regular army battalions, two Territorial Force (TF) battalions and a reserve battalion. The battalion associated most closely with the area of Dumfriesshire was the 5th (Dumfries and Galloway) Battalion TF which, on 4 August 1914, was based at Dumfries.

As in the rest of the United Kingdom, as a result of Lord Kitchener's call to arms, New Army Battalions of the KOSB were raised throughout August and September 1914, the 6th, 7th and 8th battalions all being formed at Berwick-upon-Tweed. The location of the regimental barracks at Berwick-upon-Tweed, around 100 miles to the east, may have proved a hindrance to many men who may otherwise have decided to join the New Army battalions, with Dumfriesshire men deciding instead to enlist in the 5th Battalion. The main recruiting depot of the 5th Battalion was conveniently situated at Dumfries. These geographical factors helped to ensure, that unlike many other areas of the country, in the Dumfriesshire region it was not a war-raised New Army battalion which drew most recruits, but a Territorial Force unit which attracted the greatest number of recruits and the most public support in the form of gifts and donations.

Volunteers in Langholm High Street, 1914.
Photograph courtesy of Ms Brenda Morrison and the Langholm Archive Group

The 1/5th Battalion KOSB on mobilisation, Dumfries, 1914. The soldier indicated by a cross in this photograph is Private Thomas Handford Rodgers, 1/5th Battalion KOSB, killed in action on the 12th July 1915. *Courtesy of the King's Own Scottish Borderers Museum, Berwick-upon-Tweed*

The 1/5th Battalion KOSB marching to St. Michael's Church, Dumfries, to leave the regimental colours for safe keeping, prior to entraining for Bannockburn. A church parade of the 1/5th Battalion KOSB took place and the battalion paraded in Newall Terrace; both sides of Dumfries High Street and St. Michael Street were lined with spectators. A service was held in St Michael's Parish Church, Dumfries, and a number of the battalion of the Roman Catholic Church attended a service in St. Andrew's Pro-Cathedral. A civic farewell was held in front of Dumfries Town Hall and the battalion and King's Colours were placed in St. Michael's Church for safe keeping until the battalion returned. When the 1/5th Battalion KOSB left Dumfries Station vast crowds assembled in Newall Terrace near the Drill Hall, and near the station, to bid farewell to the Battalion, as the two trains steamed out of Dumfries Station.
Courtesy of the King's Own Scottish Borderers Museum, Berwick-upon-Tweed

As the conflict continued, Dumfriesshire soldiers had opportunities to serve in a greater range of military units. Robert Irving, from Langholm, volunteered for service in the newly formed Heavy Section of the Machine Gun Corps in 1916. The Heavy Section of the Machine Gun Corps later became the Tank Corps, as can be noted from the tank badge worn above his Lance Corporal rank chevron. He was a pre-war Lanarkshire Yeomanry volunteer.

As an example of the popularity of service with the battalion, a Roll of Honour of former pupils from Lockerbie Academy illustrates the strength of the local support through recruitment for the 5th Battalion KOSB. On 26 November 1914, from a total of sixty-five former pupils enlisting for service in the Army and Navy, thirty-two enlisted into the 5th KOSB. It is also apparent from the list, that none of those volunteered for service in the New Army battalions of the KOSB. The remainder enlisted in a wide variety of regiments, the next most popular after the 5th KOSB being the Lanarkshire Yeomanry with four recruits. This support amongst the local population of Lockerbie can perhaps be partly explained by the emphasis placed on the 5th KOSB at recruiting meetings, at one recruiting meeting in the town a telegram was read by the chairman from the local members of the 5th KOSB 'wishing the recruiting meeting every success and good returns'. In the town of Moffat the popularity of the 5th KOSB was also apparent; from a total of ninety-two men who enlisted in the forces, thirty-seven joined the battalion, this being by far the most supported unit. At Dumfries, the largest town in the county, eighty men joined the 5th KOSB in a week, whilst between fifty to sixty men volunteered for service in newly forming units of the New Army in the same period.

The standing of the 5th Battalion in the region resulted in the formation of two reserve battalions, the 2/5th KOSB being formed at Dumfries in September 1914 and the 3/5th at Dumfries in March 1916. These battalions would provide replacement drafts for the 1/5th Battalion as well as taking an active role in home service.

The 3/5th Battalion KOSB, which served in the UK and provided drafts to battalions serving overseas, was the particular subject of an appeal for recruits by the Provost of Dumfries in a letter to the editor of the *Dumfries and Galloway Standard and Advertiser*. Although the battalion was classified as a Territorial Force (TF) battalion the Provost was keen to state *'all men are enlisted for general, and not for home service, so that everyone*

Regimental Pipe Band, 2/5th Battalion KOSB, January 1916.
Photograph courtesy of the King's Own Scottish Borderers Museum, Berwick-upon-Tweed

may feel that he will have an opportunity for service in the field'. The Provost went on to state: *'Military men know that members of regiments like the 3/5th have often the best opportunity of early service'*. Recruiting appeals in the local press suggest both that the 5th KOSB served as an equivalent to a New Army battalion to the area, and also help to explain its popularity in terms of the numbers enlisting.

The appeal of the battalion, confirmed by the strength of recruitment within Dumfriesshire, was also revealed by the level of public support for the troops both by individuals and the general public. A letter of thanks from the Regimental Quartermaster Sergeant of the 5th KOSB to the editor of *The Annandale Herald and Moffat News*,

2/5th Battalion KOSB, Moycullen Camp, County Galway, Ireland, September 1917.
Photograph courtesy of the King's Own Scottish Borderers Museum, Berwick-upon-Tweed

D Company, 2/5th Battalion KOSB, during the First World War.
Photograph courtesy of the King's Own Scottish Borderers Museum, Berwick-upon-Tweed

dated 4 May 1916, provides an insight into the level of support given by individuals to the battalion. Lady Buchanan-Jardine, from the Lockerbie area, sent 3,000 cigarettes

and thirty-two packets of tobacco to soldiers serving in the battalion, and the local branch of the Ancient Order of Foresters also sent a comfort parcel for each Lockerbie man serving in the 5th Battalion. This type of specific support was not given to any of the other battalions of the KOSB, or to soldiers of Lockerbie serving in other units, at this stage of the conflict.

The population of Dumfriesshire also showed support for the battalion by subscribing to a fund solely for its soldiers. Not until 1916, in the Annan area, was it decided by *The Annandale Observer* to set up a fund for local soldiers not serving in the 5th KOSB, noting that soldiers of that battalion *'have been well looked after for the past six months through the medium of the "Observer Fund"'*, the article going on to state, *'it is only*

Mascot of the 2/5th Battalion KOSB.
Photograph courtesy of the King's Own Scottish Borderers Museum, Berwick-upon-Tweed

Soldiers of the 2/5th Battalion KOSB, during the First World War. During early 1918, the 2/5th Battalion KOSB, after serving throughout the UK, and providing reinforcements for the 1/5th Battalion KOSB, was broken up. Most of the soldiers serving with the battalion at this time were posted to the 1st, 2nd and 6th Battalions of the KOSB in France. A remaining 300 men were posted to the Duke of Lancaster's Yeomanry for cyclist duty in France and the West of Ireland.
Photograph courtesy of the King's Own Scottish Borderers Museum, Berwick-upon-Tweed

natural that there should be a desire to recognise the sacrifices being made and the discomforts suffered by our boys who are in other Regiments'. By the time the general fund was set up 3,913 shillings had been contributed to the 5th KOSB fund since the start of the war.

In late 1917 a fund was established to provide plum puddings as a Christmas gift to two battalions of the KOSB, the 1/5th Battalion and the combined 7/8th Battalion. The fund was to close on the 20 October 1917, to allow time for delivery. The *Dumfries & Galloway Standard & Advertiser* and the *Dumfries and Galloway Courier and Herald* agreed, at the request of the fundraising committee, to receive subscriptions. Contributions sent to either office were acknowledged in both newspapers. Although this plum pudding collection also benefitted those serving in a New Army Battalion, the 7/8th Battalion KOSB, (the 6th, 7th and 8th Battalions of the KOSB suffered heavy casualties at the Battle of Loos in 1915 and the 7th and 8th Battalions merged in the spring of 1916) later in 1917 a collection was publicised to provide tobacco as a Christmas gift, solely to those serving in the 1/5th battalion in Palestine. In 1918, a collection for a Christmas gift of cigarettes was raising funds to send gifts to the 1st, 1/5th and 7/8th Battalions of the KOSB. By late November, £112 14s had been donated, and donations could be made at the offices of both the *Dumfries & Galloway Standard & Advertiser* and the *Dumfries and Galloway Courier and Herald*. Thus, although as the conflict continued more support was given to those serving in other units, the 1/5th Battalion KOSB remained strongly supported by the public of Dumfriesshire.

Of note, the lady is wearing a 11th 'Lonsdale' Battalion Border Regiment cap badge, just below her collar, in this photograph taken in Langholm. Unfortunately no identifying inscription accompanied this photograph.

As the numbers of local recruits for the New Army battalions were quite limited, the Somme Offensive of 1 July 1916 did not devastate the region, as was the case in many other areas of the United Kingdom. However, as a number of men from Dumfriesshire enlisted into New Army battalions, the losses of the First Day of the Somme were still felt. An example of a New Army battalion, into which several men from Dumfriesshire enlisted, was the 11th 'Lonsdale' Battalion of the Border Regiment, formed in the county of Cumberland which bordered Dumfriesshire to the south. Forming part of the 32nd Division, the Lonsdale Battalion sustained 490 casualties on 1 July 1916 advancing from Authuille Wood, near Thiepval.

Dumfriesshire soldiers serving with the Lonsdale Battalion who became casualties at the opening of the Somme Offensive included: Thomas Johnston Cochrane of Gretna; Charles Gordon Craigie of Canonbie; Thomas MacDonald of Westerkirk; Robert Moffat of Ewes; Thomas Thompson of Annan and Joseph Whyte of Dumfries, who were all killed in action on 1 July 1916.

Dumfriesshire men who became casualties serving with the Lonsdale Battalion after 1 July 1916, included James Brown Elliott of Canonbie, killed in action, 18 November 1916; John William Glendinning of Westerkirk, killed in action, 10 August 1916; Richard James Graham of Canonbie, died of wounds, 9 July 1916; John Alexander Little of Half Morton, killed in action, 14 July 1916 and Donald MacDonald of Westerkirk, killed in action, 3 December 1917.

Although the 1916 Somme offensive did not result in such widespread loss and deep mourning for the people of Dumfriesshire, 12 July 1915 became an emotive day in the local calendar. The 5th KOSB formed part of the 155th Brigade, 52nd Division and landed at Gallipoli on 6 June 1915. The attack of 12 July 1915, at Achi Baba Nullah, resulted in eleven officers and two hundred and fifty-nine men of the battalion becoming casualties, killed and wounded. Shortly after the attack of 12 July the Town Council of Dumfries sent a letter to the 1/5th KOSB Battalion Commander, Major Millar. The letter noted the bravery of the battalion, and sympathy at the losses suffered, during the attack (recorded within the War Diary of the 1/5th King's Own Scottish Borderers, WO 95/4320, The National Archives).

The content of this letter helps to demonstrate the special affinity of the area to the 5th KOSB. Furthermore, in order to commemorate the bravery of the battalion during the fighting around Achi Baba Nullah, a memorial service was held at St Michael's Church, Dumfries, in July 1916, with a large congregation attending. A similarly well-attended service was held in 1918, and the institution of the anniversary memorial service, two years earlier, was noted. Although the casualties of 12 July 1915 were not on such a horrific scale as those sustained on 1 July 1916, they had a significant impact on the local area.

Not only did the 1/5th Battalion evoke a great response from the public in terms of recruitment and commemoration of the attack of 12 July 1915, but it was also the subject of a public campaign to raise funds for a memorial to commemorate their actions. In an attempt to gain the necessary funds, during 1917, former 1/5th Battalion KOSB Regimental Quartermaster Sergeant John Scott of Lockerbie, began touring the region with a lecture detailing the battalion's service in Gallipoli, Egypt and Palestine. At his

A number of Annan soldiers of the 1/5th Battalion KOSB.
Photograph courtesy of the Dumfriesshire Newspaper Group

first lecture in Lockerbie, during December 1917, over £40 was raised, and it was noted that *'this will in no way interfere with the erection of a larger memorial to all those who have fallen in connection with the town and district'*. The erection of a larger memorial to all the service personnel of Lockerbie was a matter for the town council. This acknowledgement was in response to a letter from a member of the public noting: *'if we*

The 1/5th Battalion KOSB, leaving Stirling for Gallipoli, May 1915. Lieut. Macfarlane, in the foreground, died of wounds he suffered on 12 July 1915.
Photograph courtesy of the Dumfriesshire Newspaper Group

are going to erect a memorial to our dead heroes, let it be for them all, irrespective of what battalion or regiment they belong to'.

Although this letter shows not all members of the public had such great unequivocal support for the battalion, the fund for the memorial received a significant amount of public support, for example lectures raised £12 from Ecclefechan, £15 from Lochmaben and £7 15s from Eskdalemuir. By early 1918 £860 had been raised by Mr Scott, who had delivered his lecture seventeen times.

In 1919, a similar lecture entitled 'With the 1/5th KOSB in the East' was held in the New Hall, Kirkconnel; it was noted ex-Quartermaster Scott was well known in the area for his lectures and the Kirkconnel public were eager to learn about the 1/5th Battalion, with which seventy-five local men had served. The £25 collected from this lecture was donated to the local Comrades of the Great War. As the money previously collected from the lectures did not seem to have been spent on any form of memorial, perhaps the funds were also donated to this cause. Although the money collected was apparently not used to create a lasting a memorial to the battalion, the *War History of the 5th Battalion King's Own Scottish Borderers* is a reminder of the support the unit received in Dumfriesshire during the First World War; indeed the publication fund for the book was widely

Soldiers of the 1/5th Battalion KOSB, Egypt, 1916.
Photograph courtesy of the Dumfriesshire Newspaper Group

KOSB soldiers in the trenches at Gallipoli. The soldier in the photograph on the left is prepared for a gas attack.

Photographs courtesy of the King's Own Scottish Borderers Museum, Berwick-upon-Tweed.

supported and includes a brief summary of the assistance the battalion received from the local area during the conflict.

Following the Gallipoli campaign, the 1/5th Battalion KOSB served in Egypt and Palestine from early 1916. In April 1918 the battalion landed at Marseilles for service on the Western Front. On 11 November 1918, the unit was at Halluin, France. Following the Armistice, after a period in France and Belgium, the battalion moved, in January 1919, to the Rhineland. It was noted in the *War History of the 5th Battalion King's Own Scottish Borderers* there *'was perfect good feeling between villagers and troops, and this was characteristic of all our stay in Germany. The Rhinelanders seemed relieved to find we were not the barbarians they had been led to expect, and we, on our part, found them a kindly folk'*. The battalion remained in Germany until returning to the United Kingdom for demobilisation in October 1919.

The recruitment of public service professionals caused problems in areas of the region. In 1917 the call-up of a local doctor from Langholm, Dr Calwell, caused his patients to send a petition to the local tribunal, via Langholm Town Council, numbering 507 signatures. On 30 May 1917, the council held a special meeting to discuss the

Returning the Regimental Colours of the 1/5th Battalion, KOSB. The colours had been hung in St. Michael's Parish Church, Dumfries, while the battalion had been on active service. On 6 December 1918, the colours were handed to a colour party who had travelled from the continent to receive them. The Regimental Colours were to be taken to the Battalion, which was to be stationed in the Rhine area. The ceremony took place on the steps leading to St. Michael's Church, and was seen by many people. The colour party left Dumfries on the 6.40 pm train en-route to France. It was noted the battalion had been decimated during the war, and only around fifty soldiers of the 1/5th Battalion KOSB, who left Dumfries in 1914, remained with the battalion.
Photograph courtesy of the Dumfriesshire Newspaper Group

petition, and the sending of copies of it to the clerks of the appeal tribunal at Dumfries and the Scottish War Emergency Committee at Edinburgh. The local tribunal decided to uphold the concerns of Dr Calwell's patients and grant him an exemption from military service. However, this decision was contested at the Dumfries Military Appeal by the military representative. After much deliberation at Dumfries it was decided to direct the local tribunal at Langholm to allow Dr Calwell to serve with the armed forces. Although his services were lost to the residents of Langholm for the latter part of the war, Dr Calwell distinguished himself during 1918. Whilst serving in France with the Royal Army Medical Corps (RAMC), attached to the 13th Battalion King's Royal Rifle Corps,

On this soldier's service cap is the badge of the Royal Army Medical Corps (RAMC). In 1914 there were around 9,000 soldiers serving with the RAMC; this number increased to over 100,000 by 1918. RAMC soldiers wore round Red Cross badges on their uniform sleeves during the First World War. However, in this photograph taken in France or Belgium, these Red Cross badges are covered, as the soldier is wearing a goatskin coat. During the winter of 1914-1915, in response to the terrible conditions of trench warfare on the Western Front, leather and goatskin coats were issued. The RAMC, which treated the sick and wounded, recruited nationally and many local soldiers served with the Corps.

Local soldiers sometimes gained skills in the military which helped them to establish careers after the end of the conflict. Thomas McCracken, from Langholm, enlisted into the Army Service Corps, in 1916, aged 16. During the war he served overseas as a motor transport driver. He is pictured here (on the right) with a comrade.

he was awarded the Military Cross (MC) for tending wounded soldiers.

On 10 December 1919 the citation for his award was published in the *London Gazette*:

'For gallantry and devotion to duty during the attack on Louvignies on 4th November 1918. He attended to the wounded under very heavy shell fire and subsequently removed them to a place of safety. Later, he went through a barrage and remained dressing them in the open for two hours until all had been attended to'.

Thus, although the local community lost a valued doctor, Dr Calwell served with great courage in the RAMC.

Another valued local civil servant called up for service during the war, also from

After the war Thomas McCracken developed a successful career with the Glasgow Corporation Transport Department, eventually managing the Corporation Driving School. He is photographed here, early in his career, with a Glasgow Corporation bus.

Dr A.F. Calwell, MB, MC General Practitioner in Langholm from 1914 to 1939.

Photograph courtesy of Ms Brenda Morrison and the Langholm Archive Group

Langholm, was the local fire master. It was noted in the council minute book that Fire Master Adam, who was serving with the KOSB as a sergeant, had been replaced by Alexander G. Stewart, a local plumber. The financial cost to the council was increased by the enlistment of Fire Master Adam, as in addition to the wages paid to his replacement, the council ordered that £1.12.9 should be paid to his wife in lieu of his lost wages.

A further important local official, whose services were lost due to enlistment, was Mr F.W. Medlock, Dumfries Veterinary Officer, who was called up to serve as a veterinary officer in the army. Although an appeal was made for the release of Mr Medlock from army service, due to the risk of a fall in the standards of local meat inspections, the appeal was unsuccessful, and the local authorities did not appoint a replacement.

Chapter 2

Influences of HM Factory, Gretna

HM FACTORY, GRETNA, on which building started in 1915 as a response to the 'Munitions Crisis', was to have a huge impact on Dumfriesshire, both positive and negative. The factory, built to produce the vast quantities of cordite essential to the war effort, employed around 30,000 people at a peak, from throughout the British Empire, and stretched around nine miles from Eastriggs in the north to Mossband in the south. By the cessation of hostilities, HM Factory, Gretna had manufactured cordite to the value of £16,690,246.

As building work started during late 1915 the area first experienced an influx of workers who were employed in the construction of the factory. They were billeted in the surrounding area in great numbers and these new members of the Dumfriesshire community quickly acquired a notorious reputation. The behaviour of the labourers employed in the construction of the factory, and subsequently the factory workers, resulted in the State Control of Licensed premises from June 1916. In the area of State Control surrounding the factory, where workers were billeted, it was to have a significant impact on the drinking habits of workers, and also on the premises which were taken over by the authorities.

As an example, the Central Hotel in Annan was taken over by the Government under the Defence of the Realm (Liquor Control) Regulations 1915. On 1 March 1916, the takeover was completed by the Central Control Board and an offer made for the hotel buildings. The sum of £2,000 in compensation was arrived at by the surveyor of the property on behalf of the Royal Commission (Northern Division). However, this valuation was not accepted, with the owner demanding £7,000 for the purchase of the hotel, made

Water Pumping Station for HM Factory, Gretna, River Esk, near Longtown.

up of £5,750 as a valuation of the premises on 30 April 1909 and £1,250 for the fittings in the hotel. This new claim was considered by the Control Board and resolved in 1920, when a decision was taken to pay £3,000 for the Central Hotel, the £1,000 increase being made in respect of the swell in trade experienced by Licensed Premises from 1916 onwards (T161/35 [File S. 2110] The National Archives). Whilst the owner of the property valued the premises at £4,000 more than the amount paid to him, the reports note the hotel did not enjoy a healthy level of trade, with the property being described as *'unproductive and has produced practically no income for the proprietor since it was first erected'*(T161/35 [File S. 2110] The National Archives).

After the introduction of State Control, by late 1916 at Langholm, labourers working at the factory were billeted in an old distillery at Glentarras several miles outside Langholm. The workers accommodated there quickly gave the road leading to the distillery the reputation of being an area off limits to the general public. The passage of the men to and from the bars of the town resulted in a newspaper noting *'a favourite walk in the evenings fast losing its attraction'*. Whilst this atmosphere was to prove inconvenient to locals wishing to walk alongside the River Esk, a tragedy on this stretch of road was to highlight the problem of the alcohol consumption of the workers living at Glentarras.

On 23 September 1916 a labourer billeted at Glentarras, Lawrence Niven of Glasgow, was drowned in the River Esk just to the south of the Skipper's Bridge. It was noted by two anglers on the opposite bank of the river that Niven and two companions were engaged in talk and laughter, with a considerable amount of swearing but no quarrelling. But, shortly after this disturbance, Niven was dropped eight feet from the top of the wall by the road into the river. Following this incident, in which Lawrence Niven was drowned, James Stevenson and John McGory, both labourers employed at Gretna and both from Glasgow, were charged with murder. However, the judge decided to drop the

First World War era, roughly carved inscription (highlighted by chalk) on the wall below Skipper's Bridge, Langholm, where Lawrence Niven tragically died.

murder charge and instead imposed prison sentences of eighteen months on McGory and twelve months on Stevenson, due to their intoxicated states.

This incident resulting in a fatality suggests the extreme impact of the very high liquor consumption on the local community, and the associated heightened fear of attack from the intoxicated men. Less than a month after the drowning near Skipper's Bridge, the local press reported that three labourers at Gretna were involved in a disturbance in the centre of Langholm, with two men receiving convictions for being drunk and disorderly and one for assaulting a police officer. Similar problems were noted in the Dornock area where a munitions worker from Glasgow was charged with kicking a police officer whilst under the influence of alcohol. A fine of £3 or fourteen days imprisonment was imposed.

As well as the unruliness of the HM Factory, Gretna employees caused by alcohol consumption, there were also incidents of theft in the local areas by Gretna munitions workers. In April 1917 three female munitions workers were charged with the theft of several articles of clothing from two shops in the High Street, Annan, including four blouses, a pair of shoes and eight pairs of socks, with all three offenders receiving fines for their crimes.

The public order problems related to the factory were so severe that it was decided to take action with the creation of a Special Police Area around the factory in 1917; the Order from the Secretary of State for Scotland took effect from 1 June 1917. The force was made up of police officers from both England and Scotland. Once sworn in, the police officers could act either in England or Scotland in the Gretna Special Area, irrespective if they were from Dumfriesshire or Cumberland. In Dumfriesshire the Special Police Area included Annan, Dornock, Gretna Green, Springfield and Kirkpatrick Fleming (HO45-10959-328532, The National Archives). Thus it covered a wide area which did not include factory sites, but which housed munitions workers. It should be noted that the Special Women's Police Force, which was created to manage any problems with female workers, did not operate in the Dumfriesshire area outside the Gretna Township. Their duties were largely restricted to the factory, the Gretna Township and Carlisle.

The Chief Constable of the Cumberland and Westmorland Constabulary said, after his acceptance of the scheme, *'I have reason to believe, however, that the Dumfries Police Authority are likely to oppose the scheme as far as their area is concerned'.* In response to this acceptance it was noted on 26 April 1917 *'the line taken by Cumberland will greatly help the Scottish Office to get the Dumfries people to see reason'* (HO45-10959-328532, The National Archives), indicating hostility in Dumfriesshire to the plan. However, it was decided to alter the proposals somewhat to try to accommodate the Dumfriesshire Constabulary. Initially it was planned to make the core of the force of thirteen policemen from Cumberland and twelve from Dumfriesshire. However, these numbers were altered to nine and seventeen respectively, to give the Dumfriesshire Constabulary definite control over the area (HO45-10959-328532, The National Archives).

Although this change was made to improve Dumfriesshire Constabulary's control over the scheme, and the force was created in response to the increased levels of crime and public order incidents, the County Council of Dumfries continued to oppose the decision. It was noted in October 1917 that:

> 'After careful consideration the standing joint committee and county council are unanimously of opinion that the proposed constitution of this special police area and police force by an Order is unconstitutional, and is not warranted by any reason adduced to the police authorities of the county or their deputation. The proposal is most unsatisfactory to the police authorities of the county as they believe it will be to the ordinary inhabitants of Dumfriesshire proposed to be included in the special police area.'

When this statement was made it could possibly be considered that the council was trying to deny the problems which HM Factory, Gretna created, or was trying to defend the work of the local constabulary. However, one interesting point is that the Special Police Area meant that the Home Office would cease to pay the Chief Constable of Dumfriesshire his sizeable annual allowance of £85 towards the upkeep of his car (HO45-10959-328532, The National Archives).

Considering the high level of crime, with numerous assaults, thefts and public order problems, in retrospect the creation of the Special Police Area appears to have been justified. The decision to create the Special Police Area must also be balanced with the fact that during September 1915, the County Council in Dumfries decided to increase the number of police in the Gretna area by thirty men, this increase still obviously not ensuring the enforcement of law and order in the surrounding area. A letter from Annan Burgh Council to the Officer Commanding the Military Guard at Dornock, when dealing with a disturbance at Dornock station stated:

> 'The Police Constables on the spot had great difficulty in dealing with the offenders – the more so seeing several hundred people of the type to which the offenders belonged were assembled on the platform – and had it not been for the timely assistance rendered by soldiers from Dornock who were also on the platform at the moment, a serious state of matters may have arisen. The Magistrates have therefore instructed me, on their behalf and on behalf of the police, to express their deep indebtedness to these soldiers who voluntarily assisted in preserving law and order in the circumstances above narrated'.

This incident suggests that the imposition of the Special Police Area in the area, of which Dornock was part, was warranted, as local law enforcement measures proved to be rather inadequate at times. The Gretna Special Police Area Order of 22 May 1917 was not revoked by the Secretary of State for Scotland until 27 March 1920. Therefore the protests of the County Council in Dumfries, and the constabulary, made prior to and after the imposition of the order had no bearing on the final decision, or the length of time the Special Police Area was in operation.

In addition to the increased burden on the local constabulary, HM Factory, Gretna also put pressure on other key local services in Dumfriesshire. In Annan it was noted that the local Gas Company was unable to continue to make gas, essential for public lighting, as the stokers were on war service with the 5th Battalion KOSB. Advertisements for replacements in the local press were unsuccessful due to the lack of accommodation caused by an influx of thousands of workers for the Gretna munitions factory, the local council noting: *'The difficulty in securing men at the present time arises no doubt through the establishment of the Munitions Works in the neighbourhood of the town'* .

The provision of education in the area of Springfield was also seriously compromised by the arrival of construction workers and employees to the factory, many of whom also brought their families to the area. Mr A.S. Neill, the Head Teacher of Springfield School, wrote: *'No. on roll 186. . .and school is seated for 136'.* Two months later it was noted that *'Overcrowding gone now that Township School is open'*, suggesting the measures put in place in the area ensured the eventual return to normality for the local education system.

Although the arrival of workers resulted in an increase in crime, the rise in population had positive financial implications for local businesses in the Gretna area. Once the factory had been completed the influx of workers meant that the government could command very high rents for shop premises in the Gretna Township due to the guarantee of high levels of trade.

Rents of up to £86 13s were charged for the small shops in the Gretna and Eastriggs Townships (MUN 4/6284, The National Archives). Although this rent level could be afforded by the shopkeepers whilst trade was brisk during the war, once the war ended and the workers moved away, payment became difficult for the shopkeepers of the area. By 31 January 1923, arrears of £202 19s 6d were recorded for 117 to 119 Central Avenue, Gretna, which was used as a café, grocery and general merchants (MUN 4/6284, The National Archives). The situation was little better in Eastriggs, with trade falling. However the businesses there seem to have been able to keep up their repayments, the maximum arrears as of 31 January1923 being the Butchers at 1, The Green, with arrears of £16 (MUN 4/6284, The National Archives). Whilst these financial difficulties were apparent, it must be remembered that during the 1916–1918 period these business could comfortably afford to pay rents of up to £86 13s per year, thus indicating that the factory and the arrival of workers to the area proved to have had a positive impact on local trade, particularly during the 1916-1918 period.

When considering the overall impact of HM Factory, Gretna, many factors need to be considered, as positive and negative consequences were experienced in Dumfriesshire.

**Chimney of the Ether Plant of
HM Factory, Gretna.**

Anna Tudhope is photographed (front left) with fellow munitions workers at Gretna, during the First World War. She travelled from her home town of Langholm to Gretna by train; special trains ran daily for munitions workers. Prior to the First World War, in Dumfriesshire, women worked in a range of industries, including agriculture and mill based textile production; HM Factory, Gretna provided higher paid employment opportunities. *Photograph courtesy of Ms Janice Aitken*

Chapter 3

Wound dressing production and Red Cross Auxiliary Hospitals

THE FIRST WORLD WAR resulted in vast numbers of casualties as a result of incessant shelling, machine-gun fire and gunshot wounds. A number of specific medical challenges were also faced including gas poisoning, trench foot and shell shock.

An appropriate medical response was required and the Royal Army Medical Corps (RAMC) chain of evacuation started at the front line. A Battalion Medical Officer, his orderlies and stretcher-bearers initially attended to casualties at the Regimental Aid Post. Casualties would then pass through an RAMC Field Ambulance unit. After assessment, casualties could then be moved to a Casualty Clearing Station, which was usually situated about 20 kilometres behind the front lines, between the front line and the base area. Transportation to a Casualty Clearing Station was by horse-drawn or motor ambulances.

A Casualty Clearing Station was the first line of surgery and the furthest forward of the nursing staff, but treatment could still be limited. The holding capacity at a Casualty Clearing Station was about four weeks. This allowed soldiers to be returned to their units or be transferred by ambulance trains or inland water transport to a hospital. The severity of many wounds challenged the facilities of the Casualty Clearing Stations; as a result their former locations are indicated by military cemeteries.

If further treatment was necessary casualties could be transferred to hospitals in the base area such as Etaples, Boulogne and Rouen, where general hospitals functioned like civilian hospitals, having all specialist departments. Bacteriological and x-ray units were also attached. The holding capacity in the base hospitals allowed a patient to remain there until fit to be returned to their unit or to be transported across the English Channel, via hospital ship, for specialist treatment, or to be discharged from the armed forces.

Dumfriesshire produced the materials for wound dressings, used throughout the casualty evacuation process, in the treatment of wounded soldiers. Sphagnum moss was gathered from the hills of the area. From a depot at Beattock, near Moffat, it was noted in 1916, that more sphagnum moss was being sent to headquarters in Edinburgh, than from any other point in the south of Scotland. In one day over 400 sacks of dried moss had been sent from Beattock and Belgian refugees assisted with the picking of the moss. During 1917 at Beattock approximately 16,000 sacks of sphagnum moss were gathered, with 847 sacks dried and dispatched and 39,100 dressings dispatched.

In Moffat, the Young Women's Christian Association started a sewing room for the production of muslin bags for sphagnum moss dressings. The Rev. C.H. Dick allowed the use of the lesser hall of St Mary's United Free Church and five sewing machines were lent to the volunteers. Some volunteers also took bags to sew at home. The sewing room was open every Wednesday and Saturday from 3pm–9pm. When finished, the muslin bags were sent to the Rev. Adam Forman at Beattock.

In Lockerbie, a meeting to establish a committee to co-ordinate the picking of sphagnum moss was convened by Provost Laidlaw. Prior to August 1918 the work was carried out by the Trinity Church work party in their church hall, and they requested that an effort be made to establish a larger meeting in Lockerbie. In response to the urgent appeal by the Red Cross Society for more sphagnum moss a weekly meeting was held to carry out the vital work.

In Lochmaben fifty-two sacks of sphagnum moss were prepared for despatch by the Lochmaben Voluntary Aid Detachment (VAD) in a shop in Bruce Street. This was the third such consignment to be sent to Edinburgh by the unit and was co-ordinated by Nurse Anderson. The moss was collected on the Hightae Moss, and the Commandant, Miss Seton-Wightman of Courance, defrayed the cost of carriage. Thanks were also given to Mr Rogerson of Mossgrove who transported the moss from Hightae Moss to the depot in Lochmaben; to Mrs Rogerson, for the preparation of tea; and to the many local farmers who provided sacks.

Sphagnum moss also grew on the hills in the Langholm area. In late 1916 a letter, sent to Mrs Maud Miesegaes, was published in *The Eskdale and Liddesdale Advertiser*. Mrs Miesegaes, of Longwood was the Honorary Secretary of the Eskdale Sphagnum Moss Supply organisation. The letter was written by Sister May Paterson of 23rd Casualty Clearing Station, France; Sister Paterson had been Mentioned in Despatches by Sir Douglas Haig. In the letter she noted her unit was supplied with sphagnum moss dressings by the British Red Cross Depot, and how the Casualty Clearing Station in France had probably unknowingly used many bags of sphagnum from Eskdale. The letter closed with an appeal for more sphagnum moss:

> 'I think the size you sent very suitable, and a size slightly smaller would be very useful too. None of the sphagnum dressings are as smooth and nice as the ones I received from Langholm.'

Work parties for the Eskdale sphagnum moss dressings were held on Tuesdays, Thursdays and Fridays from 2.30pm to 4.30pm, at Chalmers Hall, Charles Street (Old), Langholm. Also published were extracts from several letters of praise received in 1917, from the War Dressing's Supply (Sphagnum Moss), 87 Palmerston Place, Edinburgh, which noted the quality of the dressings received from the Eskdale area, including the fifty large dressings, 18 inches by 18 inches, sent by special request to Edinburgh. At this time, an appeal was made for the collection of more moss from the moors as the winter supply was finished; once collected it was to be delivered to Provost Easton, Mr James Morrison, the Chalmers Hall and Langholm Distillery.

Around Langholm several fundraising activities were also organised to help to fund the sphagnum moss work. In late 1916 a concert was held in the Buccleuch Hall, Langholm, organised by Mrs Miesegaes. The concert comprised songs, choruses, duets, plays and tableaux which raised £61 5s 6d, at that time a record for a Langholm concert. In 1918, at Longwood, near Langholm, Mr and Mrs Miesegaes organised a garden fete, including flower and fruit stalls, archery and a band, which raised almost £172.

A few days after the garden fete at Longwood, a concert was held in the Temperance

Hall, Langholm. This raised £16 for the Eskdale Sphagnum Moss Supply, and was organised by Lieutenant Lee and Private Humphry. At the close of the concert, Provost Easton noted the funding position of the Eskdale Sphagnum Moss Supply, which received no government assistance; the income for 1916–1917 was £187 3s 6d and the expenditure, which was nearly all for muslin, was £234. There was thus a deficit of £47 and demand for Eskdale dressings was still great, the quality of which the Edinburgh depot noted as the best.

After the cessation of hostilities the public appeal for assistance with sphagnum moss dressings continued, this appeal being in response to questions from volunteers, enquiring if the need for dressings would cease. It was noted *'demand for these dressings is at this moment far greater than the supply and will continue urgent for some months to come'*. The notice went on to state there were *'many serious cases which will require dressings for months'* and all workers were asked to *'continue their efforts undiminished as long as the necessity continues, and we want more workers at once to enable us to meet the immediate demand for dressings'*. Volunteers continued to meet at Chalmers Hall, Langholm, from 2pm–4pm on Tuesdays, Thursdays and Fridays. In early 1919, it was noted the work had ceased and, during the conflict, Eskdale had contributed over 73,000 dressings.

After the outbreak of war in 1914, the British Red Cross and the Order of St John of Jerusalem united to form the Joint War Committee; this was to combine their resources of money and personnel, with maximum efficiency, under the Red Cross emblem. The Joint War Committee assessed the premises which were offered as temporary hospitals and those found to be suitable were established as auxiliary hospitals. The auxiliary hospitals were attached to central military hospitals, which instructed the transfer of patients, the patients remaining under the command of the military. Often ladies in the

Lady Ewart's Red Cross War Work Party, August 1916, making wound dressings from sphagnum moss collected on the hills around Langholm.
Photograph courtesy of Ms Caroline Brisbane-Jones-Stamp

Provost Cairns, Earl Haig and the Duke of Buccleuch, Langholm High Street, 1920.
Photograph courtesy of Ms Brenda Morrison and the Langholm Archive Group

neighbourhood of auxiliary hospitals served voluntarily on a part-time basis; however it was frequently necessary to supplement the volunteers with paid employees, such as cooks. Male volunteers also assisted, for example, with the transportation of patients. Local doctors provided medical supervision, which was typically provided on a voluntary basis.

The patients in auxiliary hospitals were usually the less severely wounded, and those recovering. The auxiliary hospitals were administered and staffed by local Voluntary Aid Detachments which were established in 1909 by the British Red Cross and the Order of St John of Jerusalem at the request of the War Office. The Voluntary Aid Detachments were initially intended to support the medical services during times of war but it was quickly found that the detachments could provide support during peacetime. Members, known as VADs, were trained in first aid and nursing. During peacetime VADs developed their skills by assisting in hospitals, dispensaries and providing first aid at

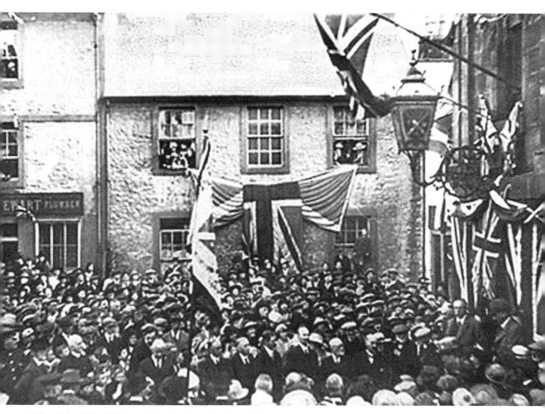

The visit of Earl Haig to Langholm, October 1920. When Field Marshal Earl Haig visited Langholm in October 1920, Provost Cairns specifically mentioned, in a summary of Langholm's war contribution, the work of the sphagnum moss workers, under Mrs Miesegaes, who made thousands of wound dressings. Provost Cairns also mentioned the Langholm Red Cross Auxiliary Hospital, under Lady Ewart, which received over 800 patients. In response, Earl Haig noted the splendid way in which Langholm had aided the comfort of the troops and the great reputation the Red Cross Auxiliary Hospital had during the war as one of the best in Scotland. Finally, Earl Haig thanked Langholm for the very warm welcome.
Photograph courtesy of Ms Brenda Morrison and the Langholm Archive Group

public events. Volunteer numbers increased significantly during the early years of the First World War; there were over 90,000 British Red Cross VADs by 1918.

As was the case throughout the United Kingdom, auxiliary hospitals were established in Dumfriesshire to assist with the treatment of wounded and recuperating soldiers.

In Sanquhar, **Eliock Red Cross Auxiliary Hospital**, with twenty-six beds for convalescent soldiers, was established by Mr and Mrs McConnel. Mrs McConnel was the hospital commandant. In the spring of 1916, twenty-four wounded soldiers were patients and the Rev. J. Richmond Wood of Sanquhar conducted a service in the hospital. It was felt that the patients were *'deriving considerable benefit from the bracing Nithsdale air'*. Early in 1916 lists of patients arriving at Eliock Auxiliary Hospital were included in the local press and the varied units they had served with is apparent. In late April 1916 patients had served with the Army Service Corps, the Norfolk Yeomanry, the North Staffordshire Regiment, the Royal Inniskilling Fusiliers, the South Lancashire Regiment, the Lancashire Fusiliers and the Royal Army Medical Corps.

In July 1916 a picnic was organised by the employees of McGeorge's Glove Factory in Sanquhar, to which the patients at Eliock Auxiliary Hospital, and local soldiers at home, were also invited. The picnic was to take place at Kemps Castle in Euchan Glen but due to poor weather the event took place in the public hall, at which well over a hundred people assembled. Several of the most unwell patients were driven from Eliock to the venue. Mr R.G. Gracie, organist of the parish church, and several members of the company, provided music. After tea, there was an afternoon of songs, dancing and indoor games. Draughts and domino competitions were arranged for the wounded men who were less able to participate in the activities. Pipes, tobacco and cigarettes were given to the soldiers, and it was noted the discharged soldiers, dressed in civilian clothes, were treated equally to the soldiers in uniform. The event ended at around 9pm, and was organised by a committee of ladies from McGeorge's Glove Factory, with Miss MacMillan, manageress, as convener.

During spring 1917 patients and staff from the hospital organised a concert in

Member of 34th Voluntary Aid Detachment (Dumfries), during the First World War.
Photograph courtesy of Ms Caroline Brisbane-Jones-Stamp

Sanquhar Public Hall, for the local branch of the Soldiers' and Sailors' Families Association, to pay the rents of men who had enlisted and, as they were not employed at the local collieries, did not get their houses rent free. Mr and Mrs McConnel had supported the cause, and when it became known funds were needed, the patients and nurses at Eliock suggested giving a concert during which £36 was raised.

In July 1917 a children's fete was held, on behalf of the Red Cross funds, in the grounds of Eliock, which several hundred children attended. The various activities for the children, such as hoop-la and football, were looked after by convalescent soldiers and nurses from the auxiliary hospital. Tea was served on the lawn for children, and adults had refreshments in the hospital, where a concert also took place. The school children contributed four pence for admission and refreshments which helped the fund substantially.

In the spring of 1918 the Sanquhar VAD held a musical concert evening in Sanquhar Public Hall. The concert was to raise money for the Red Cross and the local soldiers' comforts funds. The hall was filled to capacity with a number of wounded soldiers from Eliock Red Cross Auxiliary Hospital attending. At the close of the concert it was noted £50 had been raised, a record for Sanquhar, and the musical performers were accorded a vote of thanks on the motion of Mr J.I. McConnel of Eliock.

At Glen Stuart House, Kinmount, Cummertrees, the **Glen Stuart Red Cross Auxiliary Hospital** was established. The house was offered for use by Mrs Charles Brook and the interior was adapted to make it suitable for hospital accommodation. The first patients from hospital in Stobhill arrived in February 1915. The twelve patients arrived at Annan Station on the 5.40pm train and were greeted by a large number of cheering people at the station. They were met by Miss Brook of Kinmount; Sir Geoffrey Barton of Craigs, Dumfries; Miss Downie, Commandant of the Annan Women's Voluntary Aid Detachment (VAD); Mr W.R. Robertson Commandant of the Men's VAD; and local VADs. The patients were taken by car to the hospital, where they were met by Mrs Brook and, after tea, the patients adjourned to the smoking room. The patients were under the care of the Annan Women's Red Cross VAD.

Lists of gifts received by the hospital were published which on one occasion included

Eliock Red Cross Auxiliary Hospital, Sanquhar. *Photograph courtesy of Mr Duncan Close*

Eliock Auxiliary Hospital.

£1 3s 6d from the employees of Corsehill Quarries (their third donation to the hospital); 3s from Miss Steel of Annan; £1 from Dr Chalmers of Charlesfield; bananas, vegetables, scones, cigarettes, games, jellies, apple tarts, shortbread, magazines and papers. During 1916 the lady members of Powfoot Golf Club entertained patients from Glen Stuart Red Cross Auxiliary Hospital with tea, a putting competition and a variety of games. The afternoon was drawn to a close with the presentation of prizes to the winners.

In response to the increasing number of casualties, during early 1917, Colonel Brook, of Kinmount, arranged to provide Kinmount House for hospital use, and to make Glen Stuart the family residence for the duration of the war. Glen Stuart provided for twenty-eight patients, and the use of Kinmount House was to increase the accommodation available at least threefold. The work to convert Kinmount House into six wards and staff accommodation started immediately.

By July 1917 **Kinmount House Red Cross Auxiliary Hospital** was in operation and had sixty-six beds with Miss Buchanan as Superintendent. In the grounds a Red Cross Week fundraising fete was held. This was organised by Mrs Brook, Miss Buchanan and the VADs of the parishes of Annan, Cummertrees, Dornock and Lochmaben, with assistance from Provost Foster and the people of Annan. The patients from Kinmount, and also Castle Milk Red Cross Auxiliary Hospital, participated in the fete. Entertainment included open air concerts on the landing stage at the lake, which had been converted into a temporary platform; fruit, flowers, cakes, china, sewn items, tobacco, cigarettes and ice cream were for sale and a range of entertainment was provided until 9pm. In 1918, a similar Red Cross fete was held at Kinmount. In Annan the afternoon was observed as a holiday, and many people from Annan attended the event at which over £1,200 was raised.

During 1918 concerts involving performances by patients from Kinmount Auxiliary Hospital helped to raise funds for the Red Cross. Concerts took place in the Victoria Hall, Annan, Cummertress Hall and the Girls' Patriotic Club, Ednam Street, Annan, the concert at the Girls' Patriotic Club raising £7 15s. The concerts were organised by Miss Brook, Kinmount, and involved sketches and music. Later in the summer, some patients from Kinmount gave a concert in the YMCA Institute, Annan, which was filled to capacity; by this time it was noted the Kinmount patients had gained a *'great reputation as first-class entertainers'*. After the concert the patients were given refreshments by the association. In October 1918 between fifty and sixty wounded soldiers from Kinmount Hospital were entertained to music by the members of Annan Girls' Club, in the Girls' Hut, Ednam Street. Mrs Gemmell, manageress of the hut, presided.

In 1919, when the hospital had closed, the members of the VAD who had worked at the hospital were entertained with dinner at the Powfoot Golf Club Hotel, followed by a dance in Powfoot Hall. Colonel Brook, of Kinmount, presided at the event. He said the VAD members could be proud of their work all their lives, and wished them long life and happiness.

In September 1919, a letter was published in a local newspaper from Mr P.C. Houston, who had served as a Company Quartermaster in the Royal Scots Fusiliers. The letter was addressed to Mrs Brook and the staff at Kinmount Red Cross Auxiliary Hospital, to thank them, and all those involved with the hospital, for their kindness and work to ensure the comfort of the patients.

In March 1920, it was announced, that Mrs Mabel Frances Brook, Commandant of Kinmount Red Cross Auxiliary Hospital and Vice-President, Dumfriesshire Branch, British Red Cross Society, had been appointed a Member of the Civil Division of the Most Excellent Order of the British Empire for services in connection with the war.

Moffat Red Cross Auxiliary Hospital was established at the Proudfoot Institute. The Institute was placed at the disposal of the Red Cross by its trustees and an appeal was made for donations and furniture for the outfitting of the building. Patients suffering from rheumatism were to receive free mineral baths arranged by the town council, and Mr Hope-Johnstone, of Annandale, allowed free use of the mineral spa to patients for drinking purposes. A short time later it was reported that Mr McIntosh Bell and his brother placed their adjoining property of 2, Mansfield Place, at the disposal of the Red Cross, for use connected to the hospital. Several billiards tournaments were organised in Moffat Auxiliary Hospital. In January 1916 donated prizes were cigarette cases and leather wallets and in June 1916, a silver cigarette case and a fountain pen were donated as billiards tournament prizes.

Entertainment in Moffat was organised for the convalescent and wounded soldiers at the hospital, in the Baths Hall, which included music and dramatic sketches. Also in the audience were officers and staff of the VAD, members of the families of soldiers on active service and Belgian refugees. In the autumn of 1917 a detachment of orderlies from Moffat Auxiliary Hospital helped to gather the potato crop in a field beside Ballplay Road, which had been given to the hospital by Mr Fraser of Holmfield, Moffat.

On the closure of the hospital in early 1919, a presentation of a silver salver and two bon-bon dishes was made to Mrs Younger, Commandant of the hospital and County

The Billiard Room in Moffat Red Cross Auxiliary Hospital.
Photograph courtesy of Ms Barbara Janman

Moffat Red Cross Auxiliary Hospital.
Photograph courtesy of Ms Barbara Janman

Staff at Moffat Red Cross Auxiliary Hospital. *Photograph courtesy of Ms Barbara Janman*

Vice-President of the Red Cross. Members of the VAD and hospital staff attended the presentation. At the opening of the event the opportunity was taken to present a local soldier, Corporal Scott, Machine Gun Corps, with the Military Medal (MM), for bravery in the field. The presentation was made by Colonel Younger. Dr Park, of Vicarlands, made the presentation to Mrs Younger. Dr Park noted the role Mrs Younger played in the

A ward in Moffat Red Cross Auxiliary Hospital. *Photograph courtesy of Ms Barbara Janman*

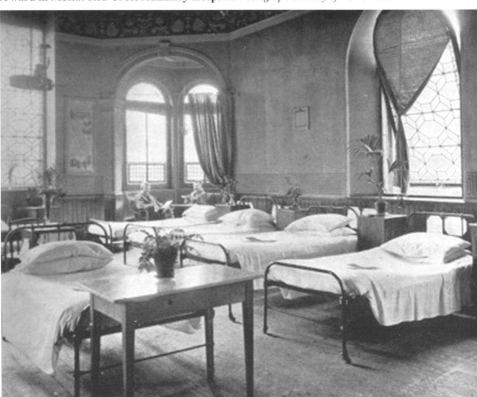

Patients and staff at Moffat Red Cross Auxiliary Hospital.
Photograph courtesy of Ms Barbara Janman

organisation of the Red Cross in upper Annandale, not only in the Moffat area, but also in the parishes of Kirkpatrick Juxta and Johnstone. In response, Mrs Younger said:

> 'they could not regret the closing of a hospital which meant, she hoped, the termination of a cruel war. But she knew many of them would miss the work, and they would all part with deep regret from the matron and sisters, who had helped to bring so much sunshine and happiness to the hospital'.

Near Thornhill, in Nithsdale, the Duke of Buccleuch offered a portion of Drumlanrig Castle as **Drumlanrig Red Cross Auxiliary Hospital**. Initially accommodating around twenty-five patients, it was managed by the Dumfriesshire branch of the Red Cross. The urgency of the need for hospital provision was shown, as just days after approval as an auxiliary hospital, eight patients arrived at the castle. In the summer of 1915 some of the patients took part in a bowling competition on the green and in the recreation hall, residents of Kirkconnel provided a musical entertainment evening.

From the opening of the hospital on 27 February 1915 to 17 July 1915, 192 patients were admitted. The total cost during this period was £602 14s 11d, a cost of 16s 7¾d per patient, per week. This sum included laundry, medical stores and all the wages paid from hospital funds. The government grant for the same period totalled £358 6s and many local parish councils contributed to the running of Drumlanrig Auxiliary Hospital in this period including Glencairn, £94; Kirkconnel, £32; Durisdeer, £20; Closeburn,

£5; Dunscore, £10; Sanquhar, £30; Wanlockhead Committee, £3 3s; Morton, £27 13s 8d; Keir, £30 18s and Tynron, £20.

In the nearby village of Moniaive, entertainment was organised by members of the Glencairn Red Cross VAD. Around twenty patients together with hospital staff were transported to the field, the use of which had been granted by Miss Moon of the George Hotel for an afternoon of sport, including five-a-side football and a potato race. A tug-of-war was a highlight of the afternoon, in which eleven of the patients were pitted against twenty-two of the nurses; after a hard struggle the nurses had the best of three pulls and were declared the winners. During the afternoon tea was provided by the nurses. Before the sports were concluded Private Jowett of the 5th Scottish Rifles proposed a vote of thanks to the Glencairn nurses for their great kindness, on behalf of the patients and staff of Drumlanrig Auxiliary Hospital. At the end of the sports, prizes including pipes, tobacco, cigarettes and chocolates were given out by Miss Macmillan, Commandant of the Glencairn VAD. The journey back to Drumlanrig was started at about 6.30pm.

By early 1917 at Drumlanrig the number of patients had increased to over forty, and the accommodation was being enlarged to accommodate up to seventy-five patients, the necessity for more space reflecting the increasing number of casualties. There was also a continued need to raise funds for the hospital, and events were held in the area around Drumlanrig. At Moniaive a whist drive in the village hall raised over £25 for the hospital funds.

At Morton Parish Hall, Thornhill, patients from Drumlanrig Castle, together with VAD nurses, organised a variety concert well attended by local people. Fellow patients from Drumlanrig also attended and were accompanied by the Hospital Commandant, Mrs Ralston and Matron, Miss Clouston. A total of £32 was raised for the hospital.

In the autumn of 1918 patients and staff at Drumlanrig celebrated the approaching marriage of Sister Campbell. Sergeant Broadford presented Sister Campbell with a silver rose bowl on behalf of the patients. Mrs Ralston, Commandant of the Hospital, and the Rev. C. Rolland Ramsay, Chaplain, also spoke.

The hospital remained open in early 1919 and entertainment continued. At Morton Parish Hall in Thornhill, a victory concert was held by patients and nurses from Drumlanrig Red Cross Auxiliary Hospital. The programme was a humorous mix of performances and was enjoyed by a crowded audience. Later in January 1919, the patients and nurses from the hospital visited Sanquhar Public Hall, where they were welcomed by the local VAD, who had prepared tea for them. The patients and nurses then gave a similar concert to that which they presented at Thornhill the week before. At the close the people of Sanquhar and Kirkconnel were thanked for the generous support they had given to Drumlanrig Red Cross Auxiliary Hospital, since it was opened more than four years earlier. It was planned to donate half of the £40 collected to the Sanquhar soldier's memorial fund. Once the concert was over the patients and nurses had tea and returned to Drumlanrig by car.

In March 1919 Drumlanrig Red Cross Auxiliary Hospital was closed. At the time of the closure there were still sixty-five patients, and it was decided to officially close the hospital to allow time for their relocation. To mark that occasion VADs connected with the hospital, permanent staff, officials, and all patients at the hospital at that time, gathered for a presentation evening. This comprised of a concert, supper and dance which over 180 people attended, including about 120 members of the Voluntary Aid Detachments of Burnhead (Dunscore), Moniaive, Sanquhar and Thornhill. Nurses and patients took part in the concert, which was a mix of music and recitations. Mrs Ralston, the hospital commandant, made several gift presentations including to Dr Bryson, the medical officer at the hospital; Miss Clouston, the matron; Miss McHaffie, quartermaster; Miss M.G. Macmillan, assistant quartermaster; Mrs Maguire, cook; the Rev. Ramsay, Chaplain and Mr James Fergusson, stoker. Several gift presentations were then made to the hospital commandant, Mrs Ralston, by representatives of the local VADs. Finally, gifts were presented to Miss Clouston, the Matron and to Sister Menzies by Sergeant Major Fergusson on behalf of the patients. During his remarks about the great work of the hospital, Sergeant Major Fergusson commented he had first heard about Drumlanrig Hospital whilst in the trenches at St Quentin. After tea in the dining room, a dance was held in the recreation hall which lasted until midnight.

During the four years Drumlanrig Red Cross Auxiliary Hospital was open, around 2,190 patients received care there.

In 1917 the Matron, Miss Emma Margaret Clouston, was awarded the military decoration, the Royal Red Cross, 2nd Class, in recognition of her valuable service in connection with the War.

Patients and staff at Drumlanrig Castle Red Cross Auxiliary Hospital, 1916.
Photograph courtesy of Dumfries and Galloway Photographic Archive, Ewart Library, Dumfries, Ref. Da 4 (362)

Patients and staff at Drumlanrig Castle Red Cross Auxiliary Hospital, 1916.
Photograph courtesy of Dumfries and Galloway Photographic Archive, Ewart Library, Dumfries, Ref. Da 4 (362)

Langholm Red Cross Auxiliary Hospital was established early in the conflict by the Langholm VAD under the leadership of Lady Ewart of Craigcleuch. The hospital was established in the Parish Church Hall, to which some slight alterations were made. Once complete the hospital had a ward, an office, storeroom, kitchen and lavatories. An initial inspection of the facilities was made by General Sir Geoffrey Barton of Craigs, accompanied by Dr Maxwell Ross, Medical Officer of Dumfriesshire. It was noted that although the Langholm VAD was one of the last to be formed in Dumfriesshire, it was second to none in efficiency and had the satisfaction of being the first to have a temporary hospital occupied by wounded soldiers. At the time of the inspection, eleven patients were in the hospital, all wounded in the fighting on the Aisne. Additional patients were expected to arrive from Edinburgh the same evening.

In October 1915, to celebrate the first anniversary of the opening of the hospital, a concert was held and the generous and loyal support of the people of Langholm and district was noted. During this first year the hospital had treated over 184 wounded and sick soldiers from France, the Dardanelles and home service. By 1917 the number of sick and wounded having passed through the hospital had risen to 400. A Christmas tree function and concert took place at which Lady Ewart and Miss Ewart donated gifts for

Langholm Red Cross Auxiliary Hospital. This postcard was written in 1918 by a nurse to a former patient.

the patients, staff and Boy Scouts; a musical concert also took place. In early 1918, Langholm Red Cross Auxiliary Hospital was again inspected, this time by Colonel Wallace CMG, who was most satisfied with the hospital and arrangements for the wounded. Also in early 1918, a list was published, thanking local people for their

Langholm Red Cross Auxiliary Hospital, Christmas 1917.
Photograph courtesy of Ms Caroline Brisbane-Jones-Stamp

generous donations, which included apples, cigarettes, crackers, soap, socks, magazines, haggis, milk, eggs, seats in the local cinema and cars to transport patients from the station to the hospital. On 16 October 1918, the hospital celebrated its fourth anniversary. Almost 700 sick and wounded soldiers had passed through the hospital in the four years since it was established. A concert was held to celebrate in which patients and staff took part. At the concert's close, on behalf of the patients, Rifleman Dyball thanked Lady Ewart and her staff for their work.

Towards the end of the year it was announced that the hospital was to close on 31 December 1918 after constant devotion to sick and wounded soldiers since it opened on 16 October 1914, with twenty beds. Members of staff who served a long period included: Lady Ewart, Commandant and donor; Miss Charlotte Matheson (Certificated Nurse) Matron; Miss May Ewart (VAD), Quartermaster; Miss Bessie Cairns (VAD), Cook; Miss Margaret B. Scott (VAD), Nurse; and Miss Kitty Ellis (VAD), Nurse. The Medical Officer was Dr Calwell of Langholm. At the closing of the hospital, Lady Ewart received a communication from the War Office warmly thanking her, and the staff, for their assistance to wounded soldiers.

Christmas tree, Langholm Red Cross Auxiliary Hospital. *Photograph courtesy of Ms Caroline Brisbane-Jones-Stamp*

Patients and staff at Langholm Red Cross Auxiliary Hospital.
Photograph courtesy of Ms Caroline Brisbane-Jones-Stamp

Staff at Langholm Red Cross Auxiliary Hospital.
Photograph courtesy of Ms Caroline Brisbane-Jones-Stamp

Members of the 34th Voluntary Aid Detachment (Dumfries) with patients, outside Langholm Red Cross Auxiliary Hospital. Two patients in RAMC uniform are sitting at the front with round Red Cross badges on their sleeves. *Photograph courtesy of Ms Caroline Brisbane-Jones-Stamp*

Patients and staff at Langholm Red Cross Auxiliary Hospital, May 1916, standing on the right, is a patient in Royal Flying Corps uniform. *Photograph courtesy of Ms Caroline Brisbane-Jones-Stamp*

Patients and nurses from Langholm Auxiliary Hospital at Craigcleuch, July 1917.
Photograph courtesy of Ms Caroline Brisbane-Jones-Stamp

In 1922 a presentation was made to former staff of the hospital, by General Sir John Spencer Ewart of Craigcleuch. The presentations took place in Langholm Parish Church Hall which had been the hospital. General Ewart felt either the Victory Medal should have been awarded to all who contributed to victory, home or abroad, or a special medal should have been issued for home service. Red Cross War Service Medals were awarded to Lady Ewart, Dr Watt, Mr Thomson, Mrs Burnet, Miss Cairns, Miss Lottie Cairns, Miss Ellis, Mrs Fletcher, Miss Hyslop, Miss M.B. Scott, Miss Frewing, Mrs Williams, Mrs Watt, Miss Mercer, Mrs T. Scott, Miss M.E. Scott, Mr T. Bell and Councillor A. Armstrong. Several people entitled to the medal were unable to be present and others, such as Dr Calwell and Mr Adam Grieve, could not receive it due to their award of other medals for overseas service. Congratulations were also extended to Dr Calwell on his award of the Military Cross.

At St Mungo Hall, Kettleholm, near Lockerbie, the **Castle Milk Red Cross Auxiliary Hospital** was established by Lady Buchanan-Jardine of Castle Milk, who was the Dumfriesshire President of the Red Cross Voluntary Aid Detachments. St Mungo Hall was built in 1907 by Sir Robert W. Buchanan-Jardine for use by the local community. The hospital was entirely furnished and equipped by Sir Robert and Lady Buchanan-Jardine, who also employed a trained nurse as superintendent. The hospital duties were carried out by the St Mungo Women's VAD, of which Miss Alice Jardine Dobie was commandant, assisted by the St Mungo Men's Section, led by Mr Rafferty. The hospital included a ward, dining room, kitchen and bathroom, amongst other facilities. Dr Maclachlan of Lockerbie was the medical officer and visited the hospital daily.

Some of the earliest patients at the hospital were seventeen Belgian soldiers, most of whom were wounded in the battles around Diksmuide in 1914. They were recovering from shock and bullet wounds and Belgian newspapers were provided for them. The recovering Belgian troops also enjoyed motor trips around the area, due to the kindness of Lady Buchanan-Jardine, Mr Aitken of Norwood, Mrs Bell-Irving of Milkbank and Miss Jardine Dobie of Gyleburn. In November 1914, the Lockerbie Girl Guides arranged a musical concert, and one of the patients, M. Joseph Boulanger gave an excellent rendition of *Je sais que vous êtes jolie*. By mid-December, eleven Belgian soldiers left Lockerbie by train, nine to Folkestone and two to London. In early 1915, the remaining Belgian soldiers recovering at Castle Milk sent a letter to be published in the local press, thanking all those associated with the hospital for their care and for the hospitality shown to them during the Christmas and New Year celebrations.

As the war continued more patients arrived at Castle Milk Hospital. In March 1915,

Patients and nurses from Langholm Red Cross Auxiliary Hospital.
Photograph courtesy of Ms Caroline Brisbane-Jones-Stamp

Hospital staff preparing meals for patients of Castle Milk Auxiliary Hospital.
Photograph courtesy of Sir John Buchanan-Jardine, Bt.

fourteen wounded and invalided soldiers arrived from Stobhill, under the charge of Sergeant McGavin, RAMC and Sergeant McKay, RAMC. They were met in Lockerbie by local VADs and were welcomed to Kettleholm by Lady Buchanan-Jardine and other hospital staff. Later in the year, eight wounded men arrived from Stobhill and an equal number of convalescents left the hospital, and eleven wounded, including a sailor, arrived from Stobhill in the charge of Sergeant Dunlop, RAMC.

Concerts and entertainment were regularly held for patients. During the spring of 1915, patients from the Red Cross Auxiliary Hospital at Glen Stuart, Kinmount, arrived at Castle Milk, and joined patients there for a concert and tea. A garden party, to which patients at Glen Stuart were also invited, was held at Castle Milk later in the summer.

At the opening of the season at St Mungo Bowling Club, it was announced that the patients at Castle Milk Hospital were given free membership. In the autumn of 1916, the patients organised a concert, the hall being completely filled despite stormy weather. Patients and nurses gave a concert of music and comic sketches and £17 15s was raised for the Red Cross Society. Later in the year, patients and staff from the hospital held a concert in Lockerbie Town Hall also in aid of the Red Cross Society. The programme included short sketches, songs and dances. A matinée for children was held the previous afternoon. The concert was well attended and the proceeds amounted to £28 12s 3d.

In the winter of 1917 a concert was held for patients by the local Scouts and several patients also took part. The following spring another concert for patients was held at Kettleholm by the St Mungo Choir and some patients also performed.

In early 1919 Castle Milk Red Cross Auxiliary Hospital was closed. A presentation was held in which St Mungo VADs and hospital staff presented their Commandant, Lady

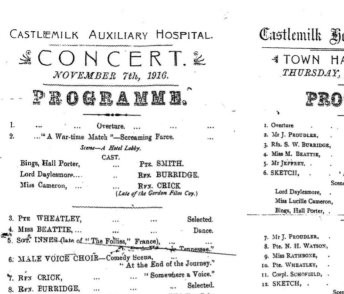

Castle Milk Red Cross Auxiliary Hospital Concert Programmes.
Courtesy of Sir John Buchanan-Jardine, Bt.

Buchanan-Jardine, with an illuminated address contained in a curio table. In a speech Dr Maclachlan, spoke of the kindness and generosity of Lady Buchanan-Jardine, since the hospital opened on 3 November 1914. Although there was great thankfulness that the fighting had ended, and there would be no more wounded to treat at Castle Milk, there would be a little sadness as the hospital had become the centre of interest for the members of the VAD and the local community. A presentation of a vanity bag was made to Sister Doig, on behalf of the VADs, by Dr Maclachlan. Lady Buchanan-Jardine presented Dr Maclachlan with a gift from Sir Robert and herself, a personal gift to Sister Doig and the staff, a small brooch as a memento to all the VADs, and a pin to each member of the men's VAD. Those present at the closing meeting were grateful to Mrs Aitken for arranging the event marking the end of their connection with the hospital, which would long remain a pleasant memory for all who worked there. During the time Castle Milk Red Cross Auxiliary Hospital was open, 700 patients had passed through.

In 1919 Miss Nora Paterson, Sister, Castle Milk Red Cross Auxiliary Hospital, was

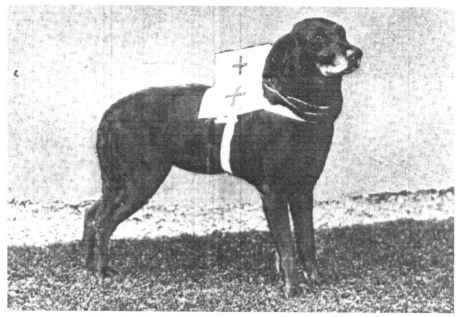

A dog at Castle Milk collecting for the Red Cross. *Photograph courtesy of Sir John Buchanan-Jardine, Bt.*

awarded the Royal Red Cross, 2nd Class, in recognition of her valuable nursing services rendered in connection with the War.

In December 1916 **Lockerbie Red Cross Auxiliary Hospital** was opened in Lockerbie Volunteer Drill Hall, in response to the national appeal for more auxiliary hospital accommodation. The Drill Hall was fully equipped and handed to the Lockerbie VAD by Sir Robert and Lady Buchanan-Jardine, who had already opened the Auxiliary Hospital at Castle Milk. The main hall was converted into a ward with sixteen beds and the upper floor was equipped as a recreation room for patients. At the rear of the hall a bathroom and sanitary facilities were added. Kitchens, dining room and staff quarters

Patients and nurses in the dining room (Lesser Hall), Castle Milk Red Cross Auxiliary Hospital. *Photograph courtesy of Sir John Buchanan-Jardine, Bt.*

Patients and nurses in the Nursing Ward (Main Hall), Castle Milk Red Cross Auxiliary Hospital. *Photograph courtesy of Sir John Buchanan-Jardine, Bt.*

were created in the adjoining instructor's house. The hospital was managed by the Lockerbie VAD, with Mrs Hunter of The Hill, as Commandant. The medical officer was Dr Maclachlan, of Lockerbie, and the Matron, Miss McBayne, of Edinburgh, who had experience in the South African War and had just returned from eighteen months Red Cross service in Rouen, France. Like the hospital at Castle Milk, convalescent patients

Apart from regular maintenance, St Mungo Hall has seen few changes since being built in 1907. The Hall remains a local community asset. Photographed in 2014.

were transferred to Lockerbie Auxiliary Hospital from Bellahouston Hospital, Glasgow.

In early 1917 a whist drive was held in Lockerbie Town Hall by the Lockerbie Ladies' Tea Party Committee to support the hospital. The prizes were donated by Captain W. Dobie of Broombush and there was a large attendance. The prizes were presented by Miss McBayne, the Matron. Donations were regularly received by the hospital and were published in the local press. They included bed socks, butter, oranges, tea, haggis, socks, turnips, cheeses, shirts, scones, cakes, eggs, cigarettes and subscriptions to various weekly magazines.

During 1918 presentations of the Military Medal to patients took place. Corporal Carney, Royal Engineers, received his MM from Lieutenant Colonel Maclaren for saving the lives of four soldiers in an explosion during an enemy mining attack. There were a large number of people present including Lady Buchanan-Jardine, soldiers from Castle Milk Auxiliary Hospital and local VADs. Later in 1918, Private J. Luke, Royal Scots Fusiliers, was presented with the MM for rescuing wounded soldiers on 21 October 1916, during the Battle of the Somme. Whilst acting as stretcher-bearer he tended numerous cases between the front lines under heavy shell and rifle fire. The ceremony took place on the hospital lawn, in the presence of patients, Sister Donald and the local company of Volunteers, under the command of Lieutenants Hunter and Bell Irving. Lieutenant Hunter presented the MM to Private Luke.

In November 1918 a concert was held in Lockerbie Town Hall in aid of the funds of Lockerbie Hospital. Arranged by patients and friends in Lockerbie, it was noted *'owing*

Lady Buchanan-Jardine in the centre of a group of patients and staff at the Castle Milk Red Cross Auxiliary Hospital. *Photograph courtesy of Sir John Buchanan-Jardine, Bt.*

Red Cross helpers at the side door of the Castle Milk Red Cross Auxiliary Hospital, with the corner of the Post Office House, Kettleholm, in the background. Mr Rafferty, the local schoolmaster, is in the front of the group. *Photograph courtesy of Sir John Buchanan-Jardine, Bt.*

to the good news from the front everyone was in good spirits'. All the convalescent soldiers from Castle Milk and Lockerbie hospitals were present, as well as some local soldiers on leave. Over £40 was raised.

Lockerbie Red Cross Auxiliary Hospital was closed in early 1919, and remaining wounded soldiers were transferred to Bellahouston Hospital, Glasgow. To mark the closing a presentation evening was held, at which the local VADs were present. On behalf of the nurses, Dr Maclachlan presented gifts to Mrs Hunter, Commandant; Miss Jardine, Quartermaster and Sister Donald, Matron. The Rev. J.G. Grieve, of All Saints' Church, gave a vote of thanks and tea was served followed by an evening of song and dance.

In October 1914 in the county town of Dumfries, **Dunbar Terrace Red Cross Auxiliary Hospital** was established. The house of the late General Tweedie, 3 Dunbar Terrace, was placed at the disposal of the Red Cross VAD; the detachment was supervised by Dr Maxwell Ross, County Director. The hospital was initially furnished to accommodate twenty patients, but provision was made to accommodate about another twenty if necessary. Staffed by seventy Red Cross nurses under the supervision of a resident trained nurse, Dr Laidlaw was the medical officer. Several wards were created including one with six beds for seriously wounded soldiers confined to bed. On the second floor there was a linen store. The commandant's office was located near to the entrance and sitting and sewing rooms were provided for the nurses. Two bathrooms were incorporated into the second floor and on the ground floor a dining room, pantry and kitchens. A recreation room provided a piano, gramophone and writing material. Spacious grounds surrounded the hospital and the entrance was in the lane next to Elmbank.

During late 1914 a detailed list of subscriptions to the hospital was printed, together with the collectors of the donations. A total of £279 3s 1d was acknowledged in this first list of subscriptions.

In the summer of 1915 six new patients had arrived at Dunbar Terrace Hospital from Glasgow. They were met at the station by Mr D. McGeorge and Mr A.C. Penman, and were transported by motor car. Later in 1915, Canon O'Brien donated £15 to the hospital from proceeds of entertainment given in Brooke Street Hall by the children of St Andrew's School.

In December 1915 Surgeon-General W.L.M. Price of the Army Medical Staff inspected the hospital and he expressed his great satisfaction. Gifts to the hospital included bread, cakes, scones, cigarettes, jam, tea, daily papers and a whist prize. Similar lists of gifts to the hospital were published regularly although from June 1916, due to the charge made for printing the lists, acknowledgements were only made monthly in the press.

During the summer of 1916, the arrival of eight patients brought the number of patients to thirty, the full complement for the hospital at that time.

In December 1917 the members of St Mary's Church choir provided entertainment for the patients. Around ninety people attended the concert, including forty-five patients. The programme consisted of songs, dances, games, tea and supper. Later in December, the patients, together with the VAD nursing staff, were welcomed to a Christmas dinner and dance in the dining hall of the Queensbury Hotel. The total number of guests was 110, of whom forty-five were wounded soldiers. Mrs Kirk, of the Queensbury Hotel, organised the event, in association with the VAD. The sum of £22 10s was raised by three prize draws.

During February 1918, the employees of the Arrol-Johnston aero wing section held a social evening in the Masonic Hall, which involved music, refreshments, dancing and whist. Earlier in the year, the Arrol-Johnston aero wing section had also arranged a very successful Burns Night for Dunbar Terrace hospital patients.

In spring 1918 St John's Church choir visited the hospital to entertain the convalescents with songs, recitations and readings. More practically, in May, a gift of eighteen dozen eggs was sent to the hospital, collected by the children at Glencaple School. Later in 1918 the patients enjoyed a night of song and dancing organised by the South United Free Church Cycling Club in the hospital recreation hall. The entertainment lasted from 7pm to 2am, with refreshments served at 10pm, and was organised by Mr Thomas Freeman, convener of the party, who was assisted by the visiting ladies and gentlemen and Private A.S. Allen, South Lancashire Regiment, a patient. The evening was particularly happy, as it was the first entertainment at the hospital following the Armistice.

In December the patients at Dunbar Terrace were entertained at the canteen of the Arrol-Johnston Works, Dumfries, an event organised by the employees of the machine shop. Following tea, the patients enjoyed a musical evening, including songs, sketches and a dance. The entertainment was noted as *'one of the most lavish and generous of its kind ever provided for the enjoyment of the convalescent soldiers in the Dumfriesshire district'*.

On Christmas Day the patients were each given a gift at breakfast time, followed by lunch and Christmas dinner in the evening, which was enjoyed in the dining room seasonally decorated with bunting and evergreens. Following dinner, on behalf of the patients, Private Goodchild thanked the staff and management of the hospital for all the good things they had provided and Mrs Stewart for cooking the Christmas dinner. He concluded by calling for a vote of thanks for the Matron, Miss McKenzie; and for Mrs D. McGeorge, Mrs Henderson and Miss Dickson. Musical entertainment and dancing followed in the hospital recreation room until after midnight.

In early 1919 the 'Y' Branch of the British Women's Temperance Association entertained the patients at Dunbar Terrace hospital with supper, dancing and games. Patients also contributed to the musical entertainment, the entertainment closing at around 1am.

By February, Dunbar Terrace hospital was to be closed. The patients and staff held a fancy dress ball, organised by Mrs Henderson and the staff of the 46th Voluntary Aid Detachment, which was one of the nursing units at the hospital. Over fifty patients and nurses appeared in costumes and prizes were awarded for the best fancy dress; music and dancing followed in the hospital recreation hall.

When Dunbar Terrace Red Cross Auxiliary Hospital closed, the Commandant, Mrs D. McGeorge, entertained members of the nursing staff, and their friends, at a social evening in the Royal Restaurant. Nearly 200 guests enjoyed a dance and whist drive, followed by presentations; the nurses present wore their hospital uniforms. Presentations

Dumfries Voluntary Aid Detachment, Dunbar Terrace Red Cross Auxiliary Hospital, Dumfries. *Photograph courtesy of Ms Caroline Brisbane-Jones-Stamp*

Member of 34th Voluntary Aid Detachment (Dumfries), during the First World War.
Photograph courtesy of Ms Caroline Brisbane-Jones-Stamp

were made to Mrs McGeorge, Commandant; Miss McKenzie, Matron; Mrs Henderson, Commandant of the 46th Voluntary Aid Detachment; Miss Dickson, Quartermaster; and Dr Glover, Medical Officer. Mr D. McGeorge, Dock Park House, presided over the presentations, and among those present were Provost and Mrs Macaulay, the Rev. J. Montgomery and Dr J. Maxwell Ross, County Director of the Red Cross Society.

During several speeches the support received from the people of Dumfries was praised, as was the fact that the hospital had not needed to request financial support from the county. It was further observed that the Government grant at first was 2s per head per day and as time went on, the grant was increased to 3s. At the time of the closing of the hospital the grant was at 3s 3d per head per day, and some pride was taken in that the hospital had been run without needing to apply for the maximum grant due to the many gifts received from the people of Dumfries, including goods and money. The rent-free status of the building was also of great financial assistance, to which the hospital was indebted to Mr James Henderson, solicitor and agent for the trustees of the property. The furniture and other items provided on loan were returned to donors. The electrical appliances and some other purchased items were donated to Dumfries Infirmary for the treatment of discharged servicemen. Other items were sent to the Industrial School, the Nurses' Institute and the Girls' Home. Following the presentations

Patients and nurses from Langholm Red Cross Auxiliary Hospital, in the garden of Langholm Old Parish Church Manse, 1918. *Photograph courtesy of Ms Caroline Brisbane-Jones-Stamp*

Patients from Langholm Red Cross Auxiliary Hospital, at Craigcleuch, 1915.
Photograph courtesy of Ms Caroline Brisbane-Jones-Stamp

there was music and dancing, a whist drive and a buffet.

From December 1914 until it closed on 28 February 1919, Dunbar Terrace Red Cross Auxiliary Hospital treated 1,069 wounded soldiers. It was staffed by four Voluntary Aid Detachments: Mrs McGeorge's (No. 14), Mrs Henderson's (No. 46), Mrs Hutcheon's (Locharbriggs) and the men's detachment, with Mr Adam Black as Commandant.

In March 1920 it was announced Mrs Mary McGeorge, Commandant of Dunbar Terrace Red Cross Auxiliary Hospital and Vice-President, Dumfriesshire Branch, British Red Cross Society, had been appointed a Member of the Civil Division of the Most Excellent Order of the British Empire for services in connection with the war.

It was announced in 1918 that a number of ladies associated with Red Cross Hospitals in Dumfriesshire had been brought to the notice of the Secretary of State for War, by the Chairman of the Joint War Committee of the British Red Cross Society and Order of St John of Jerusalem. These included: Miss E. Cairns, Langholm Auxiliary Hospital and Miss I. McHaffie, Drumlanrig Auxiliary Hospital *'for valuable services rendered in*

Members of 34th Voluntary Aid Detachment (Dumfries), with patients of Langholm Red Cross Auxiliary Hospital, Lady Ewart, Commandant, seated middle 2nd row. *Photograph courtesy of Ms Caroline Brisbane-Jones-Stamp*

Members of 34th Voluntary Aid Detachment (Dumfries), at Langholm Red Cross Auxiliary Hospital, 1915. Medical Officers Dr Gibbs (left) and Dr R.H. Watt (right). Lady Ewart, Commandant, centre back row. *Photograph courtesy of Ms Caroline Brisbane-Jones-Stamp*

connection with the establishment, organisation and maintenance of hospitals'; Miss V. Buchanan-Jardine, VAD, Nurse, Castle Milk Auxiliary Hospital; Sister Miss N. Paterson, Castle Milk Auxiliary Hospital; and Miss J.F. Mackenzie, Nurse, Dunbar Terrace Auxiliary Hospital, Dumfries *'for valuable nursing services rendered in connection with the war'*.

In 1919 Miss A. Dickson, Dunbar Terrace Auxiliary Hospital, Dumfries; Miss M.F. Henderson, Kinmount Auxiliary Hospital, Annan; and Miss M. McMillan, Drumlanrig Auxiliary Hospital, Thornhill were brought to the notice of the Secretary of State for War *'for valuable services rendered in connection with the war'*.

Chapter 4

Public celebrations

ALTHOUGH THE FIRST WORLD WAR caused considerable anguish and grief throughout Dumfriesshire, public celebrations were still supported in local communities. Two celebrations exemplifying the public spirit in the region were the celebration of St Patrick's Day and Langholm Common Riding.

A report in the local press detailed the notable St Patrick's Day celebrations of 1917, primarily held by the Irish community working at HM Factory, Gretna. At Annan, during the morning, the Irish people living in the town celebrated relatively quietly. However, as numerous workmen arrived in the early afternoon, excitement and queues grew as a number of girls started to sell green ribbons; people rushed from seller to seller and the ribbons were soon sold out. In Gretna, although no official holiday was observed, many Irish people had a holiday appearance and wore the shamrock. There was also great demand for shamrocks amongst local people. A noted positive aspect of the St Patrick's Day celebrations was that there was no sign of alcohol involved in the festivities. A concert took place in the evening.

In contrast to the quite spontaneous celebrations of St Patrick's Day in Annan and Gretna, Langholm Common Riding, one of the oldest celebrations held in Dumfriesshire, continued throughout the First World War, despite several difficulties.

Celebration is an appropriate term for the event as inhabitants of the town look forward every year to the date when the Common Riding is held. In 1919 a public meeting established the date of the Common Riding as the last Friday in July; prior to this, the date had been variable, as it was governed by the Langholm summer, or lamb, fair. It was noted at the meeting that returning soldiers supported this change of date.

At the time of the Burgh's Charter in 1621 certain pieces of land were granted as 'common' to the inhabitants. It was to check the boundaries of this common land, to ensure no neighbouring landowner had encroached upon it, that a yearly inspection was made. Langholm's ceremony dates from 1759 when the area of common land was legally determined, and its limits marked by natural features such as streams or by man-made ditches or cairns. Since 1759 Langholm Common Riding has developed into the very popular event it is today. Over the years it had associated with it the summer fair, one of the largest lamb sales in the country, and part of the Common Riding tradition is the proclamation of the Langholm Fair, by an official Fair Crier.

By the First World War, the various ceremonies associated with the event had become traditional. On the evening before the Common Riding, known as the 'Summer Fair Night', a gathering of inhabitants took place at the railway station to meet the last train by which visitors could reach Langholm in time to take part in the festivities. A procession led by the town's flute and pipe bands then went through the streets of the town. At 5am the following morning Langholm was awakened by the flute band, and

Scene in Langholm Market Place, Common Riding Day, 1901. All four of the emblems; the Spade, the Thistle, the Floral Crown and the Barley Bannock are in the right foreground. The members of Langholm Town Band, arguably the oldest in the country, have very little room to manoeuvre due to the crowd. The Cornet, carrying the Burgh flag, can be seen far left. *Photograph courtesy of Dumfries and Galloway Photographic Archive, Ewart Library, Dumfries, Ref. De 401 (394)*

1914

Langholm Common Riding, 1914.
Photograph courtesy of Ms Brenda Morrison and the Langholm Archive Group

spectators climbed the hill to watch the hound trail. Returning to Langholm Market Place, the Burgh Standard was handed over to a popularly elected Cornet, who then led a group of mounted followers up the face of Whita Hill to the town mosses and quarries near the summit. On their return to the town, the Cornet and his supporters, preceded by the town's brass band, rode through the streets. The procession also included four emblems: a large Scots thistle, a crown of flowers, a spade and a wooden platter with a barley bannock and a salt herring nailed to it.

Common Riding afternoon was taken up by horse racing, athletic events, Highland dancing and meeting old friends. In the evening, the Burgh Standard was ceremonially handed back, and the assembled crowds joined in the singing of Auld Lang Syne and the

Langholm Common Riding, 1915. Dancing on the Castleholm.
Photograph courtesy of Ms Brenda Morrison and the Langholm Archive Group

Langholm Common Riding, 1916. The children (front left) are carrying heather besoms.
Photograph courtesy of Ms Brenda Morrison and the Langholm Archive Group

National Anthem. One unusual feature of the event is that the official Common Riding colours for ties, rosettes etc are those of the winning horse in the Epsom Derby.

In 1916 Langholm men of the 1/5th Battalion King's Own Scottish Borderers had not forgotten the Common Riding held on 27 July, whilst they were serving in the Middle East. A letter from a Langholm soldier in the battalion mentioned that Lance Corporal J. Morrison was 'crying the fair'. The letter also noted the Langholm soldiers most longed for the last polka in the Market Place, when the Town's Standard was returned to the Town Hall.

During the First World War the established form of the Common Riding was disrupted. It was the accepted custom that the Cornet should be an unmarried man, and as many of the town's young men were serving in the forces, the Common Riding Committee proposed the event should be abandoned. There was a public outcry, with letters in the press from local inhabitants and servicemen protesting strongly about this decision.

In 1915 an anonymous letter from a local resident noted it was almost seventy years since they had experienced their first Common Riding. This letter, addressed to the editor of *The Eskdale and Liddesdale Advertiser*, demonstrated the strong feelings in the community in support of the event:

'Sir, I am grieved to learn that it has been decided by the guid folks of the "Muckle Toon" to abandon the Common-Riding this year. Nothing gives the Wild Beast of

Berlin greater encouragement in his mad career of deluging the Continent with blood as does the postponement of any of our British pastimes. The conceited murderer hugs himself with the notion that this is a certain sign of our faintheartedness, whereas it is nothing of the kind. The noble manner in which Langholm, Canonbie, Eskdale, Liddesdale, and Annandale subscribed to the war fund and supplied recruits to oppose our common enemy was sufficient evidence that ye were heart and soul in the business, and confident of winning the great struggle. Time-honoured institutions should never be abolished if possible; and many a young and hardy youth at the front, when the Common-Riding date comes round, will longingly think of the doings on the Castleholm.'

With this passionate support in the community, the Common Riding was held in 1915, although some of the usual events were curtailed, with no sports taking place. Mr John Wilson, the 1914 Cornet, was asked to carry out the duties again. It was noted he was the only Cornet in the past hundred years who had been chosen twice and that he would occupy a distinguished position among Cornets. The Hound Trail was run, but only over a practice trail, with no prizes being offered or entry money taken. Provost Easton did not deliver the flag to the Cornet, as he did not approve of holding any celebration; this duty instead was performed by Bailie Cairns.

On behalf of the Common Riding Committee Bailie Cairns presented Mr Andrew Johnstone, the Cornet of 1865, with an inscribed silver-mounted walking stick. It was noted not many men were able to attend the event fifty years after taking part in it. There were only twenty-one mounted supporters of the Cornet, a much reduced number, and they were accompanied by Langholm Brass Band. Hundreds of children with heather besoms also took part in the celebration. At the close of the programme, the National

Langholm Common Riding, 1917.
Photograph courtesy of Ms Brenda Morrison and the Langholm Archive Group

Anthem was sung, with Langholm Brass Band leading and, on the suggestion of the Rev. J. Buchanan, parish minister, a message was ordered to be despatched to all from the town and district serving in the military, wishing them God-speed and a happy return.

In 1916 the situation was even more serious. The local tweed mills were on full wartime production, consequently the usual holiday could not be held and the town band could not make an appearance until 7pm in the evening. The 1917 event saw an almost

'Crying the Fair', Langholm Common Riding 1918. Cornet T.G. Elliot, wearing the Cornet's sash and carrying the Burgh Flag, was the only Cornet to have worn military uniform. The Fair Crier, standing on horseback, was the Cornet's father, Christopher Elliot.
Photograph courtesy of Dumfries and Galloway Photographic Archive, Ewart Library, Dumfries, Ref. De 401 (394)

Robert McCracken, who served as a Staff Sergeant with the Royal Army Ordnance Corps during the Second World War, was very proud of the fact that, although he had not been Cornet, he had still carried the Town Flag round Whita Hill.

identical situation, with those wishing to hold the Common Riding opposed to a small minority who felt it should be abandoned. No arrangements had been made to have the Burgh flag available, and those in charge of its safe keeping refused to release it. It was declared that if the Burgh flag was not made available, then the Cornet would carry the Union Jack, it being noted as the flag being fought for in the war. However, an old and tattered town flag was found and carried by the Cornet in his gallop up the hill. It was then furled and given to a 14-year-old boy, Robert McCracken, to carry until the cavalcade returned to the town.

The last wartime Common Riding in 1918 still caused controversy, but again the event took place. Private T.G. Elliot, at home at the time, had served with the KOSB in Gallipoli, Egypt, Palestine and was twice wounded at Gaza; he was unanimously appointed Cornet. Cornet Elliot was supported by fifteen riders, including Miss Marshall, Natchill House, Canonbie, who was the first lady to ever ride with the Cornet. Some 500 children marched, carrying heather besoms, and each received a new three-penny piece. There were no horse races or sports, but the hound trail was run over a seven-mile course. The winning hound was 'Crazy Lad', belonging to Mr Baldry, Egremont, Cumberland, who won the silver cup.

The Cornet's Chase, horse race, was won by the Cornet, with Miss Marshall, finishing second. The day concluded with dancing in the evening.

The tradition of Langholm Common Riding continued during the war and the local community spirit ensured the conflict did not stop one of Dumfriesshire's oldest celebrations. After the cessation of hostilities in November 1918 the Common Riding returned to its peacetime format.

The internationally famous poet, Hugh MacDiarmid, born in Langholm in 1892, used the Common Riding as inspiration for his poem 'A Drunk Man Looks at the Thistle', published in 1926. MacDiarmid served as a sergeant in the Royal Army Medical Corps during the war. Like many other people from Langholm over the years, although he moved from the town as a young man, he delighted in returning to the town for Common Riding Day.

The spirit which the Common Riding evoked in the Langholm community was used in 1919 as an ideal occasion to present special commemorative medals. On the Summer Fair Night, the evening before the Common Riding Day, 1919, a special ceremony took place in the Buccleuch Hall, Langholm. Like many other towns and villages throughout the country, Langholm produced a

The Langholm Gold Medal, presented to those from the town who were decorated during the First World War.

tribute medal to commemorate the return of soldiers from the war. The Langholm medal was only presented to local residents who had been decorated for gallantry and took the form of a gold disc, on the front of which was an enamelled Langholm coat-of-arms.

Only twenty-three men were eligible to receive the award and the funds needed were raised by public subscription. In the presence of the Town's Provost and members of the town council, the Earl of Dalkeith, heir to the Dukedom of Buccleuch, presented a medal to each recipient present. Two of the awards were posthumous, to Captain Sidney McGowan MC, 5th Battalion KOSB and Company Sergeant Major Robert Milligan MM, 17th Battalion Highland Light Infantry.

In 1922 there was a new Common Riding ceremony, the laying of a wreath at Langholm War Memorial, which was dedicated shortly after the 1921 Common Riding. On the Wednesday evening prior to the event, the Cornet, with his right- and left-hand men, met at Langholm Town Hall, and received the Town's Standard from Provost Cairns. Led by Langholm Town Band, a large group made their way to Buccleuch Park, where the Cornet laid a wreath of red and white heather tied with black and white ribbons at the base of the Memorial. Major McAlister of The Glen, addressed the gathering and prayer was offered by the Rev. J.B. Macdonald, Chaplain to the ex-servicemen. Following this the large gathering, led by Langholm Town Band, sang the Second Paraphrase. After the Benediction, Pipers Erskine and Dalton played the lament, 'The Flowers o' the Forest' and the sounding of the 'Last Post', by Bugler Beattie, closed the ceremony.

Some of the recipients pictured at the presentation of the Langholm Gold Medal, Summer Fair Night, 1919. Pictured from left to right: James Armstrong, MM; Andrew Cowan, MC; Gavin Hyslop, MM; Robert Little, Medal of St. George (Russia); The Earl of Dalkieth; Lawson Cairns, DCM; Henry Irving, MM; John Grant, D.C.M. and Croix de Guerre (France); Thomas Warwick, MM; John Jackson, MM; and James Bell, MC In the background are Provost Easton, John Milne Home and Bailie Cairns.
Photograph courtesy of Ms Brenda Morrison

Chapter 5

Commemoration

AT THE END of the First World War there was a strong desire to commemorate those who had died as a result of the conflict. Throughout Dumfriesshire war memorials were dedicated, usually situated in prominent positions, often near a church or market place. The war memorials described in this chapter are intended to help represent the many memorials dedicated throughout Dumfriesshire.

In **Dumfries**, in March 1919, a meeting of the Provost's Committee of the town council, representatives of the parish council and of the Comrades of the Great War was held in the town hall to consider the proposed Dumfries war memorial. The meeting decided to call a public meeting to discuss and agree a form of memorial. The war memorial committee for the Burgh of Dumfries decided to ask for subscriptions towards the cost of a memorial and to raise as much money as possible. Any surplus cash was to be distributed among the neediest relatives of those who died in the conflict or those who were disabled as a result of their war service. At a meeting of the committee, in early

Dumfries War Memorial, immediately after the unveiling, 1922.
Photograph courtesy of the Dumfriesshire Newspaper Group

Dumfries War Memorial.

October 1920, it was reported that during the previous week £92 3s 6d had been donated to the fund.

The memorial was designed by a Dumfries sculptor and produced by craftsmen of the town. The figure chosen was that of a soldier of the King's Own Scottish Borderers. The memorial was produced by Messrs Stewart & Co. Ltd., granite sculptors of Watling Street, Dumfries, made from Creetown granite and cost approximately £1,400. It was decided to build the memorial on Newall Terrace, near St John's Church; however considerable differences of opinion were expressed, with a number of the committee strongly favouring Queensbury Square or King Street. The memorial was unveiled by General Sir Francis Davies KCB, Commander-in-Chief of the forces in Scotland. Around 6,000 people attended the unveiling of the memorial; the ceremony paid tribute to the 451 soldiers from Dumfries killed in the conflict, and the many who returned wounded. The occasion was even more poignant to many of those attending, as the date of the unveiling practically coincided with the tragic events of 12 July 1915, when the 1/5th Battalion KOSB sustained very heavy casualties in the Gallipoli campaign.

The officiating clergy were the Rev. J Montgomery Campbell, minister of St Michael's; the Rev. Duncan Ross, minister of Free St George's; and Canon Robertson, minister of St John's Episcopal Church. A guard of honour of around fifty local territorial soldiers was present. Custody of the memorial was accepted by Provost Macaulay on behalf of Dumfries Town Council. After the unveiling ceremony had taken place, nearly 300 floral tributes were left at the base of the memorial by relatives of those commemorated and by representatives of public organisations.

In late November 1918 a public meeting chaired by Mr John Samson, managing director of the Sanquhar and Kirkconnel Collieries, was held in **Kirkconnel** Parish Church Hall, to consider how to commemorate those from the area who had died in the war. It was noted that one man in every eight from Kirkconnel, who had fought in the war, had not returned.

At Kirkconnel New Cinema Hall in February 1919 a further meeting was held when seven designs were shown on the screen. After each had been shown twice, a vote was called for on voting papers supplied to attendees when they entered the hall. A total of 410 votes were recorded in favour of one design, with only 28 votes for the others. The favoured design was a statue base for the names of the fallen soldiers and, on top of this, the carved granite figure of a soldier; the approximate cost was £520–£550.

Also at the meeting four local soldiers, who had been decorated for gallantry, were presented with gold watches. Fifteen local men had been awarded decorations during the conflict, with two of this group killed: Sergeant J. McMillan and Lance Corporal M. Parker. Nine watches had already been presented, and beside the four presented that night, they were awaiting the return of two soldiers from military service. The four soldiers honoured were Sergeant Major John Brown, 1/5th Battalion KOSB, awarded the Distinguished Conduct Medal (DCM) for rescuing an officer and putting several machine guns out of action on 31 October 1918; Sergeant Samson Gibson, KOSB, awarded the DCM for bravery whilst carrying out reconnaissance in the River Lys area; Sergeant Walter Black, awarded the Meritorious Service Medal (MSM) for bravery in charge of forward supply dumps around Ypres; and Private John Cowan, RAMC,

Kirkconnel War Memorial, situated within the railed, triangular area of ground.

awarded the MM for rescuing wounded soldiers under heavy fire. The Rev. C. Forbes Charleson presided, and the watches were presented by Captain Samson, of Burnfoot. The meeting was told:

> 'We read a great deal about the new nobility, ladies and gentleman, receiving the OBE, but the DCM and Military Medal and these other decorations were infinitely greater honours. These were the men who did when we were talking at home.'

In April 1919 a public meeting at the Cinema Hall met to discuss the earlier decision to erect a granite statue, incorporating the figure of a soldier, now at the estimated cost of over £600. It was agreed that the mine workers of Kirkconnel would subscribe ten shillings each to the war memorial fund, and it was hoped those who were not mine workers would also give an appropriate contribution. Messrs Robertson and Graham and a colliery clerk agreed to collect the money at the miners' pay office; those who could not pay at once could have the money deducted from their pay in instalments and it was decided to publish the list of subscriptions.

The memorial was designed by Mr William Scott and Miss Scott, of the Sanquhar and Kirkconnel Collieries. Mr Scott was presented with a gold fountain pen by the memorial committee, in recognition of his valuable services; the presentation took place in Kirkconnel Cinema House. The war memorial was made by Messrs Scott & Rae, sculptors, Glasgow and positioned at the north-west end of the main street, next to the school, and the triangular piece of ground around it was landscaped with paths and shrubs. A *'handsome iron railing'* was built around the enclosure.

Kirkconnel War Memorial, commemorating eighty-four men from the parish, was unveiled by Mrs McConnel, of Eliock, in the presence of over 2,000 people. Many of those present were from New Cumnock and Sanquhar, while some travelled from areas further away. Mr McConnel of Eliock presided and a united service was held at which the Rev. C. Forbes Charleson, minister of the parish, and the Rev. Robert Sutherland, United Free Church, officiated.

Kirkconnel War Memorial which was unveiled in 1920.

Lockerbie War Memorial features a bronze figure of Victory by Henry Fehr, and is almost identical to that featured on Langholm War Memorial. The memorial was built at an estimated cost of £2,500 and was selected in open competition from a total of 120 designs submitted, the assessor of the submissions being Sir George Washington Browne, RSA, Edinburgh. The selected architect was Mr James Dunn, Edinburgh; and the sculptor was Mr Henry C. Fehr, Kensington, London. The memorial was built in the Market Square close to Lockerbie Town Hall on the site of the old Market Cross.

Lockerbie War Memorial, which commemorated 222 men who fell in the war, was unveiled by Lady Buchanan-Jardine of Castle Milk.

It was estimated that over three thousand people were assembled around the memorial for the unveiling, with every window and vantage point occupied. The relatives of the deceased were seated in front of the memorial.

As men from adjoining parishes were also commemorated by Lockerbie War Memorial, the surrounding district was widely represented. The town council of Lockerbie, the parish council of Dryfesdale and members of the Lockerbie District Committee were joined by representatives of the parish councils of St Mungo, Tundergarth, Applegarth and Hutton and Corrie. Many ex-servicemen from Dumfries and Moffat joined those from Lockerbie to pay tribute; they assembled at the Drill Hall

The unveiling of Lockerbie War Memorial, 1922. *Photograph courtesy of the Dumfriesshire Newspaper Group*

and were headed by the pipe band and a detachment of the 5th Battalion KOSB.

The ministers who participated in the service included the Rev. G.T. Wright, Dryfesdale; the Rev. W.J. Masson, St. Cuthbert's; the Rev. David Whiteford, Trinity; and the Rev. J.G. Grieve, All Saints. The Rev. G.T. Wright dedicated the memorial and custody of the memorial was accepted by Provost Laidlaw.

A large number of wreaths were placed in tribute on the memorial by relatives, public bodies and other organisations, and a detailed list of the tributes was included in the local press.

In the parish of **Canonbie** the memorial was funded by public subscription. At a public meeting it was decided that the memorial should take the form of a bronze figure at an estimated cost of £1,000. A site near Canonbie Bridge was most favoured and Mr Clapperton, a sculptor born in Galashiels, was approached and agreed to produce a model. Subscription lists were published and a total sum of

Lockerbie War Memorial.

The unveiling of Canonbie War Memorial, 25 September 1921.

£700 10s 6d was realised. Of this amount a preliminary sum of £200 was paid to the sculptor. When finally erected the memorial took the form of a bronze figure of a soldier '*in a reverential attitude upon a pedestal of rock-faced granite*'.

A full account of the unveiling ceremony, held on 25 September 1921, was given by the local newspaper. After a short service in the parish church, a procession led by Langholm Town Band, made its way to the memorial, to the finally selected site in the middle of Bowholm village, (the largest village of several in the parish of Canonbie). Here, like Langholm, the unveiling ceremony was performed by the Duke of Buccleuch. The pedestal upon which the statue stands, is of Peterhead granite, and was erected by Beattie and Co. of Carlisle. Mr Beattie, a native of Langholm, placed in the base of the pedestal current copies of *The Scotsman, The Eskdale and Liddesdale Advertiser*, two letters of correspondence in connection with the memorial and eight coins dating from 1914–1921. Subscriptions were insufficient and a Free Gift Sale was held to raise additional funds. Although £800 had already been raised, a further £500 was needed as costs had risen.

Also in Canonbie, a bronze tablet was dedicated on the north wall of Canonbie Parish Church which recorded the names of all from the parish who died, and those who served,

The unveiling of Canonbie Parish Church Memorial Tablet, October 1922.

in the Great War. The Canonbie Roll of Honour was published in the local press with an invitation for any corrections to be sent to the Rev. R.H. Kerr before 9 March 1920. After this date, no change would be possible, presumably as this list was to be sent to the sculptor. Like Canonbie War Memorial, the tablet was made by Mr Thomas J. Clapperton, sculptor, London, and cost £300. At the time of unveiling of the tablet, the centenary of Canonbie Parish Church and the semi-jubilee of the minister of the parish, the Rev. R.H. Kerr, were also being celebrated. A full account of the celebration was included in the local press together with a description of the memorial tablet and dedication. Immediately after the church service, the unveiling of the memorial tablet took place. The Rev. R.H. Kerr read the names of those who had made the supreme sacrifice; the Rev. Dr White offered prayer and performed the unveiling ceremony. Langholm Town Band also attended, and a large number of ex-servicemen were present.

Around ten miles west of Langholm and Canonbie, **Kirkpatrick Fleming** Parish Council called a public meeting to discuss the erection of a war memorial and a committee was elected to make necessary arrangements. Funds were raised in various ways, and by March 1920 the committee was considering different plans.

A sub-committee report led the committee to accept the offer of Messrs. Dods and Son, sculptors, Dumfries, to erect a *'monument with spire'*, of grey granite for a sum of £180, exclusive of lettering. As a result of a public vote a site was chosen at Toppinghead at the junction of the Annan and Carlisle roads. The site was donated, free of charge, by the land's owners, the Caledonian Railway. The memorial was unveiled on Thursday, 28 October 1920, by Mrs Graham of Mossknowe. The memorial was described as a *'handsome obelisk of Creetown Granite, twelve feet high'.* During the ceremony an appeal for further funds was made. Total expenditure to date had been £252 18s 2d, while total income amounted to £219 12s 9d, and further work on the surroundings was also planned. A decision to move the memorial was taken during the early 1970s, due to increasing traffic and the number of vehicles colliding with the memorial. It was relocated near to the parish church of Kirkpatrick Fleming.

Further war memorials, for Kirkpatrick Fleming, were a communion table and chair, made by John Leslie of Kirkpatrick Fleming, and communion cups.

A public meeting was held in **Moffat**, in the spring of 1919, to discuss options for the building of a war memorial. At a meeting of the Moffat War Memorial Fund it was decided to accept the tender of Mr A. Carrick, of Edinburgh, for a memorial, which was to cost £900. The memorial was designed in the style of a market cross and was built on what was considered to have been the site of the old market cross in the centre of Moffat. The sandstone for the building of the memorial came from quarries at

WAR MEMORIAL FUND.

DRAMATIC RECITAL AND CONCERT

BY

Mr A. E. O'DELL (Elocutionist), and Party,

IN

VICTORIA HALL, KIRKPATRICK-FLEMING,

Thursday Evening, 31st July, 1919, at 7.30 o'clock.

PROGRAMME.

—O☐O—

Piano Solo	March, "In Danger Ready," ... Mr C. W. AVERY.	Dorn
Song	"Jack Britton," ... Mr G. R. DAMERELL.	Squire
Recital...	"The Enchanted Shirt," ... Mr A. E. O'DELL.	Hay
Violin Solo	"Three Highland Airs," Mr N. M'INNES.	Murdoch
Song	"My Ain Folk," ... Mrs DAMERELL.	Mills
Recital ...	"Sentenced to Death," ... Mr A. E. O'DELL.	Carleton
Song (Humorous) ...	"Ideas," ... C.-Q.M.-S. MATHEWS.	—
Piano Solo	Overture, "Gilderoy," ... Mr C. W. AVERY.	Berger
Song	"Shipmates o' Mine" ... Mr G. R. DAMERELL.	Sanderson
Recital ...	"The Cosmopolitan Reciter," Mr A. E. O'DELL.	Original
Violin Solo	"Cradle Song" (Scotch), ... Mr. N. M'INNES.	Skinner
Song	"Comin Thro' the Rye " ... Mrs DAMERELL.	Burns
Recital ...	"Becalmed," ... Mr A. E. O'DELL.	Cowan
Song (Humorous) ...	"These Attrative Posters," ... C.-Q.M.-S. MATHEWS.	—
	"God Save the King."	

PROGRAMMES—ONE PENNY.   Accompanist—Mr C. W. Avery.

Concert programme, illustrating one of the methods used to raise funds for Kirkpatrick Fleming War Memorial.

The unveiling of Kirkpatrick Fleming War Memorial, 28 October 1920. The lady in the fur coat is probably Mrs Graham of Mossknowe, who performed the unveiling. Children of the Parish School are prominent at the front of the crowd. The Parish Minister, the Rev. J. Walker, led the dedication service. *Photograph courtesy of Dumfries and Galloway Photographic Archive, Ewart Library, Dumfries, Ref. Dd 36 (718)*

The unveiling of Moffat War Memorial, 1920. *Photograph courtesy of the Dumfriesshire Newspaper Group*

Moffat War Memorial.

Doddington in Northumberland. At the top of the memorial the coat of arms of Moffat, 'The Flying Spur', was included, together with a cross.

At the unveiling ceremony, which took place on a Sunday afternoon, many people travelled from adjoining parishes, to join the people of Moffat. Provost Huskie, in his robes, led the procession, together with local civic representatives, including bailies and councillors. There was a special area reserved for those who had lost relatives in the war. Major Murray of Murraythwaite, MP for the county, unveiled the memorial; he noted the seventy-seven names recorded on the memorial, and the places around the world where they fought. The Rev. Robert Somers then dedicated the memorial. A prayer of thanksgiving was given by the Rev. A.M. Smith and the benediction by Rev. R. Somers. At the close of the ceremony tributes were left, and around seventy wreaths were placed at the base of the memorial.

In **Lochmaben**, the war memorial incorporated a marble statute, representing a soldier of the King's Own Scottish Borderers. Mr D.J. Beattie, of Beattie & Co., sculptors, Carlisle, designed the monument and carried out the work. The estimated cost was £350. Lochmaben War Memorial was built in the Victory Park – which was gifted to Lochmaben by Sir R.W. Buchanan-Jardine – close to the parish church and Castle Loch. Prior to the unveiling ceremony a joint service was held in the parish church. The Rev. James MacGibbon MC DD, minister of Glasgow Cathedral, preached the sermon, and the various clergy in the parish participated at the service. Following the service Lochmaben War Memorial was unveiled by Lady Buchanan-Jardine; many people were gathered and businesses in Lochmaben were closed at mid-day.

Afterwards Sir Robert Buchanan-Jardine placed a casket containing biographical notes about the fallen, historical information about Lochmaben and copies of local newspapers, into a recess at the base of the memorial, which was securely sealed. The record was prepared at the suggestion of Dr Reid, a member of the Lochmaben war memorial committee, and was compiled by Mr Robert Fraser MA, headmaster of Lochmaben School. A duplicate was placed into the custody of Lochmaben Town Hall.

After the dedication a very large number of wreaths were placed at the base of the

Lochmaben War Memorial which was unveiled in 1921.

memorial, and a list of those who sent tributes was recorded in the local press.

Annan War Memorial was situated in a central position in the High Street, near to the town hall. Here a bronze figure of a King's Own Scottish Borderer was mounted on a pedestal of grey Creetown granite which weighed 14 tons.

The sculptor was Mr Henry Price, London; and Messrs J. Rae and Sons, Annan, completed the pedestal work. The total cost was £1,700.

Lieutenant General Sir Francis Davies KCB KCMG, Commander-in-Chief of the Forces in Scotland unveiled the memorial. The ceremony took place on a Sunday afternoon, and during the morning reference was made in all local churches to the occasion. It was estimated over four thousand people gathered around the memorial, including around a hundred ex-servicemen. During the ceremony the 206 names of those commemorated were read by Captain W. Cuthbertson MC and Captain J. Macdonald. A guard of honour was formed by the local detachment of the Territorial Army, under the command of Captain A.W. Scott, and behind the detachment were the Scouts, Guides, Brownies and Cubs.

The Rev. Neil McCaig dedicated the memorial and the 'Last Post' was sounded by Buglers Jardine, Johnstone and Joseph Comrie, who stood on the balcony of the Town Hall. Two minutes silence was held, and then the 'Reveille' was sounded. The Rev. A.A. Campbell, Erskine United Free Church, gave the benediction. Over a hundred wreaths were placed on the memorial by relatives of the fallen, public organisations and a large floral tribute from the ex-servicemen was laid by two disabled soldiers, Mr J.C.F. Prendergast and Mr J. Weild.

In **Sanquhar** a public meeting was held in

Annan War Memorial.

Photograph courtesy of the Dumfriesshire Newspaper Group

Annan War Memorial, immediately after the unveiling.

The unveiling of Annan War Memorial, 1921. *Photograph courtesy of Mr Bryan Armstrong*

Annan War Memorial, 11 November 1934.

December 1918 when a committee was appointed to consider proposals for a war memorial. At a keenly attended public meeting in March 1919, it was announced that the committee had decided the most acceptable form of memorial was an institute. Other proposals had included a hospital, a public hall and a monument. The committee had received a plan for an institute, designed by Mr Scott, of the Collieries, at an estimated cost of £4,500. A subscription of £2,000 had been received from the Sanquhar and Kirkconnel Colliery Company, on the condition that a small room was set aside in the building for returned service personnel and that the institute was opened free of debt. A number of other sizeable donations were received, taking the total subscribed to £2,925. To commemorate the soldiers of Sanquhar who had not returned, memorial tablets were included in the design.

By March 1920 £3,674 had been guaranteed to fund the proposed institute, of which £1,549 was already subscribed. The following month a concert was held in Sanquhar Public Hall, which raised £30 towards the cost. To raise further funds, in July 1920, a bazaar was organised in Sanquhar Public Hall by a committee of ladies, with Mrs J.I. McConnel of Eliock, as convener and Miss Waugh as secretary. The hall was brightly decorated and there were stalls, selling a range of goods including farm produce, cakes, sweets, flowers and tea. There were also games including hoop-la and a wheel of fortune. At the end of the event it was announced £871 7s had been raised.

In September 1921 Sanquhar Memorial Institute was opened. The institute cost £5,000, opened free of debt and was situated facing the main road. The building included

Sanquhar War Memorial. Unfortunately the maintenance costs of the Sanquhar War Memorial Institute became unaffordable for the local community. Consequently, a new war memorial was built on McKendrick Road, Sanquhar, and the bronze memorial plaques from the War Memorial Institute were moved there. The War Memorial Institute building was sold, used as a plastics factory, and eventually demolished during the 1980s.

The War Memorial Institute, Sanquhar. *Photograph courtesy of Mr Duncan Close*

a carpet bowling room, tables for dominoes and draughts, a comrades room, a reading room, caretaker's quarters and a billiard room, fitted with two full-sized billiard tables. The designer of the building was Mr William Scott, architect, Inglewood, Sanquhar, assisted by Miss Scott, his daughter, both of whom gave their services freely. The building work was completed by Messrs John Laing & Sons, building contractors of Carlisle.

Mrs McConnel of Eliock unveiled two bronze memorial tablets commemorating the seventy Sanquhar inhabitants who gave their lives in the First World War; their names were read by Mr William Forsyth, Town Clerk, and a secretary of the memorial committee. The tablets had fired cream enamel lettering and were positioned each side of the main entrance. Many people gathered from throughout Nithsdale, including around seventy ex-servicemen, and the ceremony followed a united memorial service in the parish church, in which all the ministers of the town participated. The service was conducted by the Rev. J. Richmond Wood, minister of the parish, assisted by the Rev. D. McQueen, North United Free Church, the Rev. James Baillie, United Free Church and the Rev. D. M. Donald, Congregational Church. A collection was taken at the service on behalf of the war memorial funds.

To close the ceremony, the benediction was given by the Rev. James Baillie; pipers played the lament 'Lochaber no more' and the 'Last Post' was sounded. Relatives and friends placed tributes below the memorial tablets and many of those gathered for the ceremony viewed the interior of the War Memorial Institute, at the invitation of Provost Tweddel.

To the north east of Sanquhar, in the lead mining village of **Wanlockhead**, the war memorial was funded by public subscription. At a well-attended village meeting in the Fraser Hall proposals for the memorial and funding were discussed. It was not proposed to ask for contributions outside the village, but any donations made by local societies would be gratefully accepted. A gift of £5 had been received from the Miners' Union and the society was asked for their opinion about possible contributions from their members towards the memorial. Mr William G. Wilson, President of the Miners' Society, noted it had been suggested to their members that each could contribute £1, with youths contributing half that amount. Very few objections had been raised, and collection was to be arranged by their secretary, Mr Thomas Gracie. Mr Wilson estimated around £190 would be collected from the Miners' Society and there would be people outside the society, and others in the village, who would considerably increase the sum. It was decided at the meeting to build a monument on a central position in the village on the School Brae. The monument was designed incorporating the figure of a soldier with arms reversed, made of white marble, mounted on a column of grey granite. It was built by Messrs Beattie and Co. of Carlisle, to commemorate the sixteen men from the village who died during the war.

The memorial was unveiled by Mr J.I. McConnel of Eliock and over a thousand people from the area gathered on the School Brae. Mr McConnel was joined on the platform by Mrs McConnel; the two local ministers, the Rev. C.P. Blair and the Rev. G.G. Ramage; Mr W.G. Wilson, chairman and Mr T. Gracie, secretary, of the war memorial committee. The Rev. Ramage opened the ceremony with a prayer, followed by the singing of the 124th Psalm, accompanied by the Wanlockhead Instrumental Band. A passage of scripture was then read by Rev. Ramage, followed by the singing of the

Wanlockhead War Memorial which was unveiled in 1920.

The unveiling of Langholm War Memorial, 27 July 1921.
Photograph courtesy of Ms Brenda Morrison

Second Paraphrase by the congregation. Once he had unveiled the memorial, Mr McConnel invited relatives of the fallen soldiers to place wreaths on the memorial. The National Anthem was sung and the Rev. C.P. Blair gave the benediction. The village band played the 'Dead March' from Saul and Bandsman A. Muir sounded the 'Last Post'.

Langholm War Memorial was also funded by public subscription. The town was divided into districts with collectors appointed for each area who appear to have made house-to-house calls to receive donations. The results of these collections were published weekly in *The Eskdale and Liddesdale Advertiser*, commencing on the 9 February 1921, and continued for several weeks. Individuals and the amount they contributed to the fund were noted and a total of £1,300 was raised. After some discussion and a public vote the site selected was the centre of Buccleuch Park. The sculptor commissioned to complete the project was Mr H.C. Fehr, London, who produced a bronze figure of an Angel of Peace and Victory, alighting on a globe. The names of the fallen were inscribed on a grey granite plinth below the angel, along with the campaign theatres of the First World War. The memorial cost £1,100 and the surplus £200 was used to erect an iron railing around the memorial and to endow a fund for future maintenance. Collections for the Langholm War Memorial Endowment Fund continued for some time; in August 1922 the sum of £20 7s 3d, including interest to date, had been contributed from a lecture in Langholm.

The Duke of Buccleuch officially unveiled Langholm War Memorial five days after the Common Riding of 1921. In his speech the Duke remarked on how appropriately the unveiling was timed, as so many Langholm people had returned for the Common Riding. He said:

'This is the time of year of your Common-Riding, which has always been a great

Langholm War Memorial, Remembrance Sunday, 2013.

event in your community, an event in which many of these men whose names are inscribed on this Memorial took their part with joy and gladness. It is appropriate, too, that so many who were born and brought up in this parish, and who have returned for the Common-Riding, should be enabled to be present on this momentous occasion'.

As a point of interest, in view of the large number of memorials built throughout the country, some duplication was inevitable. Bronze figures, similar to that featured on Langholm War Memorial, can be seen on war memorials in Colchester, Essex; Eastbourne, Sussex; and Lockerbie, Dumfriesshire, all sculptured by Henry Fehr.

Langholm Town Council applied to the War Office to be given German Army war trophies and received two machine guns and a 150mm field howitzer, no. 606, with carriage no. 122. The town also received smaller items including six rifles, a helmet, barbed-wire cutters, a water bottle, a mess tin and machine-gun filler. The howitzer was removed around the start of the Second World War, and the fate of the machine guns and other items is unclear.

In the years following the end of the First World War, as the planning and dedication of war memorials throughout Dumfriesshire took place, families and friends began to plan their own pilgrimages to cemeteries and memorials overseas. One such personal pilgrimage, to Belgium in 1931, was made to visit the final resting place of John Corrie.

John Corrie was the youngest son of Anne Corrie and the late John Corrie, of 71 Caroline Street, Langholm. Prior to the war he worked as a power-loom tuner with Messrs. R. Noble & Co., Glebe Mills, Hawick and he played rugby regularly for the Hawick 'Greens'. He voluntarily enlisted into the Lanarkshire Yeomanry, part of the Territorial Force, in 1911. Dumfriesshire men, who wished to volunteer to serve in a mounted unit, often decided to enlist in the Lanarkshire Yeomanry.

His diary, describing his service in the Gallipoli campaign, provides an insight into his experiences after the Lanarkshire Yeomanry was mobilised.

In 1915 he landed at Gallipoli with the unit, which fought in a dismounted infantry role throughout the campaign. Of the voyage to Gallipoli he noted, after leaving Devonport on 27 September 1915, the ship called at Malta for coal on 5 October; leaving on the 7th. On 9 October the ship called at Mudros, the capital of Lemos Island. He then noted on 11 October *'Left for Cape Helles, Lancashire Landing. Landed about 10pm'*.

Buccleuch Park and Langholm War Memorial. The field howitzer is prominently located by the swings. *Photograph courtesy of Ms Brenda Morrison*

Langholm War Memorial.

On 12 October he entered the trenches three miles behind the firing line and his unit was being shelled continuously.

On 28 October John Corrie received his first mail from home dated 3 October. On 7 November he entered the Eski Line trench for a week, with bombardment and an attack on the Turkish trenches at 3pm on 14 November. Later in November the winter weather at Gallipoli began. On 27 November he wrote: *'Up to Eski Lines. Ground covered with snow. Very cold wind-snow & rain all day'*. By mid-December the Lanarkshire Yeomanry moved out of the lines and on 10 December to a rest camp and into open dugouts. On the 12th he *'received a parcel from A. Elliot'* and was *'being heavily shelled'*. Two days later he received his fourteenth piece of mail from home.

On 18 December John Corrie met some of his friends from Langholm on the beach *'Irving, W. McGowan, Foster, Bob Bell, Peter Thomson, W. Fletcher and I together at beach'*. The next day he moved back into the Eski Line trench. Towards the end of the month he served as a regimental orderly and on 23 December *'shells had been flying on both sides'*. He then experienced a *'never to be forgotten Christmas Day, Turks shelling the Headquarters and what shells'*. On 26 December the Lanarkshire Yeomanry had a *'terrible day – worst dose the Turks ever gave us. Had 15 killed and 11 wounded'*.

Two days later the unit left for the rest camp and on 29 December the Lanarkshire Yeomanry was *'said to be leaving Gallipoli tonight'*. The following day John Corrie, with the Lanarkshire Yeomanry, *'left Gallipoli from 'V' (French) Beach on trawler to 'W' Beach'*.

Returning from Gallipoli, during February and March 1916, he was with the Lanarkshire Yeomanry in Port Said, the unit carrying out guard duty and mounted patrols. During quiet periods he fished in the nearby canal. On 29 March the area was hit by gale force winds and sand storms and on the following day he travelled to the 'A' Squad redoubt, fifteen miles into the desert on a light railway. On the 4 April he sailed in a small boat on the Suez Canal and then travelled to Alexandria by train.

He remained in Alexandria until 19 April 1916, when he left for the UK on board the Orient Line ship *Orsora*. On 24 April the ship stopped at Gibraltar for a day. The 26th was very cold and rough sea conditions were experienced, but land was sighted at 7.30am and at 8am the boat anchored in a bay and disembarkation took place. At 6.30pm he received a warrant to travel to Lanark and paraded at 7.15pm for a special train, arriving into Paddington Station, London, at 4.15am.

Once in London he enjoyed some sight-seeing, travelling by the Underground from Edgware Road to Trafalgar Square, seeing the changing of the guard at Buckingham Palace, the Houses of Parliament from Westminster Bridge and walking down The Embankment to Cleopatra's Needle. He took a bus down the Strand, past St Paul's Cathedral to Liverpool Street, took the underground to Marble Arch, ate lunch and then visited Hyde Park. Afterwards he took the underground from Trafalgar Square to Paddington, taking the *'sliding stairs'* at Paddington Station. He had dinner and

The Hawick Greens 1913–1914 season, John Corrie (back row, 7th left).
Photograph courtesy of Mr David Calvert

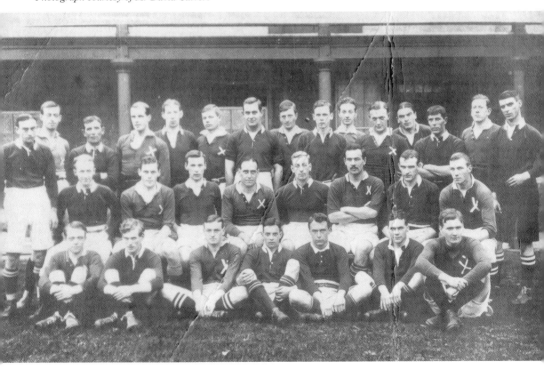

John Corrie (right). *Photograph courtesy of Mr David Calvert*

Soldiers of the Lanarkshire Yeomanry camped at Wilton Lodge Park, Hawick, September 1914. John Corrie (back row 3rd from left) and Robert Irving (front row 3rd from right).
Photograph courtesy of Mr Derek Robertson

breakfast at the YMCA and left Euston at 8.50pm on 30 April, arriving at Lanark 8am the next morning.

After arriving at Lanark, John Corrie had papers to complete and had a medical examination. Leaving Lanark at 1.40pm, he arrived at Carlisle and missed the train to Langholm by a minute. He then caught the last train to Langholm, arriving at 8.40pm, noting in his diary *'Home at Last'*.

Following his service in Gallipoli and Egypt, John Corrie had served as a volunteer in the Lanarkshire Yeomanry for as much time as was necessary to be honourably discharged from the army. Together with his friend Robert Irving, he re-enlisted into the newly formed Heavy Section of the Machine Gun Corps (which later became the Tank Corps). Robert Irving, from Langholm, served with John Corrie as a volunteer in the Lanarkshire Yeomanry from 1911, and also served in Gallipoli and Egypt.

After re-enlistment into the Heavy Section of the Machine Gun Corps, John Corrie and Robert Irving had consecutive army numbers. Both were posted to 'B' Battalion, of the Heavy Section of the Machine Gun Corps, and subsequently served in France and Belgium.

Robert Irving. Robert Irving was awarded the Croix de Guerre (Belgium) for bravery at Ypres, on 31 July 1917, and the DCM and Médaille Militaire for bravery at Cambrai, on 23 November 1917. Until his death in 1983, Robert Irving always remembered John Corrie every Armistice Day, by placing a poppy on the case containing his own decorations, which he rarely wore.

Whilst serving with 'B' Battalion, John Corrie was killed in action on 7 June 1917, age 24, during the Battle of Messines, when his tank was struck by a shell.

John Corrie's diary was returned to his sweetheart in Hawick, Lizzie Rutherford. It had been found on the Messines battlefield by a New Zealand soldier, together with a number of his personal photographs. Lizzie Rutherford's address, on the back of a photograph she had sent to John Corrie, allowed the soldier to return his diary and photographs to her.

Photograph of Lizzie Rutherford, kept by John Corrie in his diary, on the reverse of which was written her address.
Photograph courtesy of Mr David Calvert

La Plus Douve Farm Cemetery, Messines, Belgium, 12 June 1931.
Photographs courtesy of Mr David Calvert

On 12 June 1931 Lizzie Rutherford visited the final resting place of John Corrie in La Plus Douve Farm Cemetery, Messines, Belgium. She never married and when Lizzie Rutherford died in 1991, aged 96, she was buried with a photograph of John Corrie.

La Plus Douve Farm Cemetery, Messines, Belgium, 20 October 2012.

Conclusion

THROUGHOUT DUMFRIESSHIRE the impact of the First World War was felt greatly by the local communities which were decimated by the losses suffered during the conflict. The huge influx of workers to HM Factory, Gretna disrupted areas of daily life and caused an increase in crime. The population of Dumfriesshire supported those who directly suffered as a result of the war in a number of ways, including the production of wound dressings, the provision of auxiliary hospitals and fundraising efforts to provide support to refugees.

The conflict also had some positive long-term consequences in Dumfriesshire, despite the many negative impacts on the local area. One such positive consequence resulted from the building of HM Factory, Gretna, which created a great increase in demand for clean water, both for the workers at the site and also for the various production processes. The water for the Gretna Township and factory was taken from the River Esk via a pumping station at Longtown. This demand for clean water ensured Langholm, some 10 miles upstream from the water pumping station, was provided with a new sewage works. In 1917 it was noted Langholm Town Council spent £1,010 12s 10d on the sewage works for the town, this sizeable investment occurring at that time due to the need for clean water at Gretna. This had a positive impact on the health of the local population and also on the water quality downstream of Langholm.

When considering indicative key businesses, across Dumfriesshire towns, most towns experienced a negative trend in 1921–22 when compared to 1911 (see Appendix). This general trend perhaps can be explained by the shortages of produce experienced during the conflict and the loss of employees to war service. The quite significant decrease in the number of wine and spirit merchants in 1921–22, when compared to 1911 (see Appendix), can most likely be attributed to the State Management Scheme of brewing and liquor sales in the area of HM Factory, Gretna, which proved to be a lasting legacy of the conflict and was not ended until 1971.

Enduring reminders of the sacrifices made by the people of Dumfriesshire during the Great War are the annual Remembrance Day commemorations. Services of commemoration are held, and wreaths are laid, at the many memorials in memory of those who sacrificed so much in the First World War and conflicts since.

Appendix

Dumfries, Kirkcudbright, and Wigtown Trades' Directory 1911

	Dumfries	Annan	Langholm	Lochmaben	Lockerbie	Moffat	Sanquhar
Grocers	86	32	17	16	19	16	12
Tailors	22	10	5	4	7	5	5
Hotels	20	7	7	3	7	7	5
Wine and Spirit Merchants	43	5	2	0	3	4	0
Blacksmiths	12	9	8	4	2	5	6
Farmers (paying yearly rental of £30+)	38	63	13	67	33 (Dryfesdale)	29	28

N.B. Dryfesdale is the Parish in which Lockerbie is situated; all the other towns detailed formed their own Parishes.

Dumfries, Kirkcudbright, and Wigtown Trades' Directory 1921-22

	Dumfries	Annan	Langholm	Lochmaben	Lockerbie	Moffat	Sanquhar
Grocers	77 (-9)	27 (-5)	13 (-4)	11 (-5)	18 (-1)	12 (-4)	8 (-4)
Tailors	29 (+7)	7 (-3)	6 (+1)	3 (-1)	5 (-2)	1 (-4)	5 (0)
Hotels	18 (-2)	6 (-1)	7 (0)	4 (+1)	7 (0)	6 (-1)	5 (0)
Wine and Spirit Merchants	36 (-7)	0 (-5)	2 (0)	0 (0)	0 (-3)	3 (-1)	1 (+1)
Blacksmiths	10 (-2)	10 (+1)	8 (0)	3 (-1)	3 (+1)	4 (-1)	3 (-3)
Farmers (paying yearly rental of £30+)	40 (+2)	60 (-3)	12 (-1)	60 (-7)	31 (-2) (Dryfesdale)	30 (+1)	26 (-2)

N.B. Figures in ( ) relate to the difference between the 1911 and 1921–22 totals.

Bibliography

Primary Sources

Local Records
County Council of Dumfries, Minutes of Council and Reports of Committee
Langholm Town Council, Minute Book 8
Langholm Town Council, Minute Book 9
The Royal Burgh of Annan, Letter Book 6
Gretna Public School Logbook
Dumfries and Galloway Photographic Archive

National Archive Material
HM Factory, Gretna records
The London Gazette
The War Diary of the 1/5th Battalion King's Own Scottish Borderers

Newspapers
The Annandale Herald and Moffat News
The Annandale Observer
The Annandale Record
Dumfries and Galloway Courier and Herald
Dumfries & Galloway Standard & Advertiser
The Eskdale and Liddesdale Advertiser

Trade Directories
Dumfries, Kirkcudbright, and Wigtown Trades' Directory 1911, (Edinburgh: Town and Country Directories, 1911).
Dumfries, Kirkcudbright, and Wigtown Trades' Directory 1921–22, (Edinburgh: Town and Country Directories, 1922).

Secondary Sources

Adamson, Duncan and Sheila, *Kirkpatrick Fleming-On the Borders of History*, (Dumfries: Dumfries and Galloway Natural History and Antiquarian Society, 2010).
Bardgett, Colin, *The Lonsdale Battalion 1914–1918*, (Wigtown: G.C. Book Publishers Limited, 1993).
Bogle, Kenneth R., *Scotland's Common Ridings*, (Stroud: Tempus Publishing Ltd., 2004).

Bold, Alan, *MacDiarmid,* (London: John Murray Ltd., 1988).

Borg, Alan, *War Memorials*, (London: Leo Cooper, 1991).

Close, Duncan, and McGavin, Bob, *Old Sanquhar*, (Ochiltree: Stenlake Publishing, 1998).

Houston, George, (ed.), *The Third Statistical Account of Scotland, Vol. XII, The County of Dumfries*, (Glasgow: Collins, 1962).

Hunt, John, *A City Under the Influence*, (Carlisle: Lakescene Publications, 1971).

Hyslop, John & Robert, and Booth, Dorothy, *Langholm As It Was*, (Inverness: D.H. Booth and E.D. Booth, 2002).

James, E.A., Brigadier, *British Regiments 1914–1918*, (Heathfield: Naval and Military Press, 1998).

Little, Betty, *From Dawn to Dusk-The story of the Langholm Common Riding*, (Langholm: Eskdale and Liddesdale Newspapers Ltd., 1997).

MacDiarmid, Hugh, *Complete Poems 1920–1976-Volume I*, (London: Martin Brian & O'Keefe Ltd., 1978).

McCracken, Alex and Timothy, *Langholm's Roll of Honour*, (Dumfries: Private Publication, 2005).

McDowell, William, *History of Dumfries-Fourth Revised Edition*, (Dumfries: T.C. Farries & Co. Limited, 1986).

Routledge, Gordon L., *Gretna's Secret War*, (Carlisle: Bookcase, 1999).

Scott Elliot, G.F, *War History of the 5th Battalion King's Own Scottish Borderers*, (Dumfries: Robert Dinwiddie, 1928).

Behind the Parapet-The Western Front Association Scottish Branches Newsletter, March 2011.

British Red Cross information sheet-*Auxiliary hospitals during the First World War.*

British Red Cross information sheet-*What is a VAD?*

Website

RAMC in the Great War **www.ramc-ww1.com**

Index